Essential Financial Techniques for Hospitality Managers

Cathy Burgess

(G) **Goodfellow Publishers Ltd**

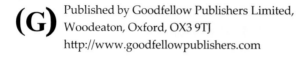 Published by Goodfellow Publishers Limited,
Woodeaton, Oxford, OX3 9TJ
http://www.goodfellowpublishers.com

British Library Cataloguing in Publication Data: a catalogue record for
this title is available from the British Library.

Library of Congress Catalog Card Number: on file.

ISBN: 978-1-906884-16-1

 Design and typesetting by P.K. McBride, www.macbride.org.uk

Printed by Marston Book Services, www.marston.co.uk

Cover design by Cylinder, www.cylindermedia.com

Contents

Foreword

Hospitality is a `people business' - but it's also a money business. No matter what sector you work in, if we don't effectively manage our revenues, costs and profits then we won't survive in an increasingly competitive and complex market place. Managing the money isn't just the responsibility of the finance department - all managers have to take financial responsibility for their area of the operation, whether it's staff, beds, food stocks or cash.

It's not difficult - in fact most of it is common sense combined with knowledge of `the business' - and any manager can make a difference. By leading from the top and setting a good example, managers can have a significant impact on driving forward revenues and building the bottom line, for the benefit of both their career and, of course, their organization.

There is no doubt that this book can help you to become a better manager and I recommend this text for all managers in hospitality who need to manage the business finances responsibly and effectively.

Paul Dukes, FCA,

Chairman of the British Association of Hospitality Accountants (BAHA), baha-uk.org

Preface

What's the point of this book?

Well, it's about money! Whether you're working for a large corporation operating in many countries or helping on a takeaway stall, if you don't manage effectively then you'll lose money. You, as an individual, are important because your actions as a manager or supervisor determine how your staff will behave. A pound saved (or made in revenue) on one transaction multiplies to a vast sum when you consider the number of transactions in a day, and repeated time after time. Thirty pounds a day is almost £11,000 a year, enough to pay your wages for several months.

The hospitality and tourism industry is enormous, employing almost two million people in the UK (about 7% of the UK workforce, and growing) in its many different sectors, all of which have their own individual characteristics. The skills you acquire in one sector can be used in another, so although you may think, for instance, that hotels are 'different', many of the features are similar. This is particularly true of the finance area, as all key activities are transferable and have an impact on the money aspect in one way or another.

Also, many financial aspects of the hospitality business are common to all industries. For the successful management of any type of business (including those that are non-profit-making) you need to address three main areas:

☐ Improving revenue

☐ Reducing costs

☐ Caring for assets.

Purpose

The purpose of this book is to give you an understanding of how your actions can affect the management of the business and the financial consequences of these actions. We will look at the different features of the various sectors, and identify many of the areas in which you can help improve efficiency and hence the financial results. You will develop an understanding of the basic principles of financial control and how it can affect the organisation as a whole.

You do need 'accounts' to help you do this. However, this isn't an 'accounting' book. Although we will be looking at some of the accounting statements the approach throughout is to look at management first and then numbers second. You don't need to be good at number-crunching to be an effective manager - as long as you can use a (simple) calculator then you will be able to work through some of the examples that are given in the different chapters. What is important is that you are able to understand the effect of your actions and those of others on the finances of the organisation.

So - the book is more of a manual that you'll be able to use both now and in the future. By the end of it, therefore, you should be able to:

☐ Understand why the 'bottom-line' is important

☐ Use some of the main techniques to control your area of business

☐ Calculate the effect of your actions in a range of real-life scenarios.

Structure

This book is divided into 11 chapters. The first two look at the importance of control, the basic accounting statements and how the statements are put together. Chapters 3 and 4 focus on the management of revenue and costs. Chapter 5 looks at pricing issues and Chapter 6 deals with forecasting future levels of business, which is crucial to planning your activities.

Managing cash and stocks appear next – two of the most susceptible areas for losses – and this leads in to standard costing which is a technique essential to sectors with exact recipe specifications, such as airline catering. Chapter 9 shows how you can utilise simple spreadsheets to help you perform all these tasks more easily. Chapter 10 then looks outside the unit and gives you an insight into how it relates to the 'bigger picture' of the whole organisation, and why different types of company structure might be relevant to you. The final chapter summarises the book, gives a brief introduction to forecasting future trends and then suggests some resources that could help you further develop your skills.

Approach

The approach is very pragmatic and 'hands-on'. You will see lots of real-life examples from a variety of industry sectors and each section will have some mini-exercises to practise so that you know how to use the different techniques. There are answers to these exercises at the end of the book.

We assume that you are working, even if only a few hours a week, so you'll also have chance to go and find out how things operate in your workplace and what makes your business function effectively (or not!). If you aren't in employment then please use a facility you know - your local pub or cafe will do fine. Also included are some useful tips. The key word throughout is control.

At the end of the book is a reading list to help you find out more about different areas. Some of these are financially-based, others focus on other disciplines or specific sectors. You will also see a list of on-line resources, and don't forget too that industry journals can be really helpful (e.g. *Caterer and Hotelkeeper* and *Hospitality*) in providing you with up-to-date industry practice and ideas about what is happening elsewhere in your own and other sectors.

Acknowledgements

With thanks to Allen, Rachel, Vicky and Tim for all their patience and support, and thanks to everyone from the industry who gave their assistance.

1 Introduction to hospitality control

- Hospitality and tourism
- Features of the industry
- Theft
- Stakeholders
- Organisation
- Accounts

Introduction

In this first chapter we will introduce the concept of 'control' and hospitality in general. We'll also look at the function of the financial control office where some of the control processes take place. As you'll see as we work through further chapters, much of control happens in the operating departments – so control is a business-wide function, not just an accounting one.

By the end of this chapter you should be able to:

■ Understand the basic approach of this book

■ Define what a business is and the main reason for control

■ Describe the main features of the different sectors of the industry

■ Describe the various activities of the financial control office.

So, what is a business?

We use the word 'business' here to mean any type of hospitality or tourism operation, whether profit-making or not. Three definitions of a business are:

☐ An industrial or commercial concern which exists to have dealings in the manufacture or purchase of goods for sale or the sale of a service

☐ An organisation which invests in buildings and equipment and pays people to work in order to make more profit for the owners

☐ As above but one which makes money in order to fulfil some type of charitable purpose.

These have been put together from a variety of sources but do give a broad outline of what a business is about. To decide which of these three is most appropriate for your area we need to look in more detail at the characteristics of the different sectors. But before that, let's look at the industry as a whole.

About hospitality and tourism

We have taken the broadest definition of hospitality, including not just hotels and catering but also tourism and leisure.

The hospitality and tourism industry is estimated to be worth about £110 billion annually to the UK economy (British Hospitality Association *Hospitality Handbook 2009*, see the BHA website). It employs about 7% of the workforce which is about 2 million people. In terms of government we are looked after by the Department for Culture, Media and Sport (DCMS) although there's input from the Department for Business Innovation and Skills (BSI) and others as well.

The Institute of Hospitality (IoH), the British Hospitality Association (BHA) and People1st are all good sources of industry statistics. The 2009 BHA *Hospitality Handbook* says that there are about 263,000 outlets, divided principally into hotels (46,000, though a lot more are thought to be unregistered, for instance small bed-and-breakfast establishments), catering in education (34,500), pubs (50,000, down by 10% in 10 years) and restaurants, of which there are about 26,000 plus 30,000 cafes and takeaways.

Some years are very good for the business although when we have a national economic crisis (or world recession, terrorist attack, very bad summer weather, for instance) this can have a widespread impact. In these circumstances people may travel less both within and to the UK, and so don't spend as much money, which means businesses can't afford as many staff. This results in unemployment or shortened hours, which in turn makes staff less willing to spend their own money on meals, travel, entertainment and so on. The whole economy suffers if hospitality activity is down.

Overall features of the industry

Commercial versus non-commercial

The industry tends to be divided into two broad categories – commercial (hotels, restaurants, fast food, pubs, transport catering, clubs, cruise ships, outside catering, tour operators) and subsidised (hospitals, prisons, education, armed services). Commercial businesses need to persuade people to buy their products and, since this relies on disposable income, customers make choices as to where they will spend their money.

On the other hand, where there is a captive market (prison, factory, airline or school meals, for instance) then you need to keep your customers happy for different reasons, whilst operating within imposed financial constraints.

Hours of operation

For many it's a 24-hour business which means that there are features and problems that don't affect many other types of industry, which may well operate on a five-day, 39-hour week and be closed on public holidays.

Other industries (and government as well, perhaps) don't always recognise the particular problems that emerge here and the costs involved. For instance, they may see a motorway service area only in the middle of the day, forgetting it needs to be open all night to provide toilets, meals and fuel, or may forget that nurses, hotel porters and crew on a ship are on duty all night and need to be fed.

Types of activity

There are different types of industry within hospitality too. There's production (like manufacturing, for instance in a kitchen), retail (a bar is like a shop) and service (restaurants, rooms).

Perishability

One principal feature is perishability in its widest sense – if the product isn't sold today then often it can't be sold tomorrow. A room in a hotel, a cabin on a cruise ship, a place on a tour or a ride on a big-dipper are all examples. The raw materials may also be perishable (such as fresh food) which means that if they are not sold then they could be wasted. Businesses may be also very seasonal – a pub in a student area, a cruise line, a summer resort – may all have peaks and troughs in trade at different times of year, as well as on different days of the week.

Features of the different sectors

Here are some of the features for a number of different sectors – you may well be able to think of a lot more.

Hotels

These are multi-unit and multi-product – rooms, food and beverage, leisure and subsidiary services. Food and beverage may be restaurants, cafes, carveries, banqueting, conferences, room service, lounge, club, vending. Hotels vary in size, in standard, in facilities offered and in length of stay. We also include in this sector simple bed-and breakfast or budget sector accommodation where few facilities are offered, and serviced apartments with hotel-style services available.

Here you see the multi-industry approach – production, retail and service all appear in one department or another. A restaurant may have all three. This complexity means that there will be many differently-skilled staff and systems.

Introduction

'Front of house' means the operating units (sales to customers) whereas 'back of house' is all the support services the customer doesn't see, such as kitchens, maintenance and accounting.

Resorts

These are even more complex – like hotels but with extensive leisure facilities and services. Some of the staff, such as sports managers, may not even consider themselves as being part of 'hospitality'. This can mean issues regarding conflict of interest or lack of awareness of guest needs.

You can often find inclusive packages being sold for resorts – the price you pay includes a room, meals, sports and perhaps beauty therapy as well.

Residential homes and hostels

These are similar to hotels in concept but provide long-stay accommodation and limited facilities, albeit with a 'home-from-home' approach. Many have only a few rooms (such as residential homes for the elderly) and so control problems are limited. The opposite is the university campus which may have hundreds of bedrooms, perhaps on several sites, where there can be problems with theft and damage.

If they offer meals (and some offer three meals a day) then they will be allowed a certain amount of money to provide these. This subsidy can be quite low if funding is given by educational or social service departments.

Restaurants (and cafes and fast food)

These provide a wide range of different types of service – from haute cuisine with full silver service to takeaways. They are often strongly branded, being either owned or franchised, and may be themed around either a product such as pizza or coffee, or a style, such as Japanese.

They can have very strong control systems where the slightest variation is noticeable. This is essential if they are situated in very expensive locations such as high streets and shopping malls.

Some menus and dishes are very complex whereas others may be very simple, depending on the type of restaurant, and food may be prepared from scratch with all raw ingredients, or bought in fully prepared.

Cafes may be 'stand-alone' or sited in museums, bookshops, supermarkets or clothes shops. They may be branded chains or use the opportunity to advertise their own products, such as own-label food or china – so although there's still a profit motive this may be for the whole store, not just the catering outlet.

Pubs

These display a great variety dependent on location – they may serve a small village, where they have an important social function, or be in the middle of a city. Traditionally they were 'beverage led' but increasingly they are 'food led' as customer habits have changed. Many modern pubs also include additional facilities such as entertainment or playbarns, to attract particular sectors of the market, or be themed ('Irish' bars, for instance).

Pubs deal with a lot of cash and handle high volumes of drink, and also have a traditionally itinerant and low-paid workforce which make them particularly prone to control problems.

Cruise ships

These are floating resort hotels, with the added complication of a ship's crew and the need to find supplies in a variety of locations. Some of the larger ships have well over 1,000 staff and 2,000 or 3,000 passengers – an enormous number of people to accommodate, feed and entertain on a daily basis.

The package that is offered to guests is usually 'all inclusive' with up to seven meals a day and most entertainment being included in the price. Although this reduces the potential problems with collecting payment it can mean very tight cost controls are needed. There are also logistical issues regarding supplies if a ship is away from port for several days.

Staff tend to work seven days a week for the period of their contract, which may be six or seven months away from home. The hospitality staff (as opposed to the ship's operating crew) may be multi-skilled and expected to help out in a range of areas.

Transport catering

This includes rail, in-flight catering, motorway service areas (MSAs), as well as cruise lines above.

You often have potential for a captive market here (although you can be competing against customers bringing their own supplies) so you need to ensure that you offer value for money. The pricing may be very tight and so strict controls are essential if the business is to make any sort of profit. There's a tendency now to offer branded products in MSAs and at rail stations.

Trains may have to offer trolley as well as buffet services, and planes a variety of food types (whether on sale or included in the fare), to satisfy differently-priced categories of traveller and a range of dietary requirements.

Leisure centres

The main function of these is to provide sporting facilities – pool, gym, squash courts and perhaps therapies – with catering as a minor part of the operation, and often generating little revenue. Some units may only have vending machines whereas others may have much more extensive catering – it depends on the location, the space and the clientele.

Contract catering

A wide range is found here, from catering for residential schools, oil rigs or universities to staff in a large city office block. Often these will have a secondary purpose in keeping the 'customers' together and encouraging team relationships and good timekeeping. Although the prices tend to be low the customers may still be very demanding in terms of quality and menu choice and may be very aware of healthy eating trends.

You may well be competing with customers bringing in their own food or going elsewhere to eat, so you need to ensure a good product and service to attract and keep your customers. More than one type of catering may also be offered as part of a single contract, such as a directors' dining room, main restaurant, coffee shop and vending. In multi-unit sites, or where there is a food court (lots of small units in one area, suitable for high volumes) there's a trend towards using high-street brands as well as in-house brand names.

Contracts can be either 'cost plus' where all costs plus a fee are charged to the client or 'fixed price' where there is a greater incentive for the operator to control costs and maximise revenues. Performance guarantees need to be put in place so that standards are maintained and costs don't rise to unacceptable levels. Others may operate on a 'nil cost' basis where the contractor does not earn a fee but gains its revenue from the discounts negotiated with suppliers – you need very high volumes and very tight cost control for this to be effective.

Contract caterers are often able to supplement the basic facility with 'hospitality services' that typically are directors' dining rooms, meeting room catering and special functions. They usually have a separate pricing structure and are additional to the standard product – and so are more profitable. Other services now being added to the contract are non-catering items such as laundry, cleaning services and shops. The length of a contract can vary depending on the type of operation and the amount of investment in facilities that each side wishes to make.

Function or event catering

These offer outside catering at events such as sports tournaments or weddings and tend to be one-off events, run at a temporary venue (such as in a marquee) with logistical problems such as having to supply all equipment as well as staff and food and drink. This may range from corporate hospitality at a sporting event to a hot-dog stall at a country fair.

There will be a small core staff but many will be employed on a casual basis for a single event, which means that their motivation for working is more to do with money than job satisfaction and career prospects. There can be lots of opportunities to cheat both the customer and operator, with a lot of high value items in transit.

Clubs

These may be licensed, where an individual runs them, or registered, where they are run by a committee. They may offer lower-priced services in return for an annual membership fee. If run by a committee then they may be run as not-for-profit, so the main purpose is to provide a service for members and to cover costs. Without a professional management approach there may be losses that the committee isn't aware of.

Hospitals

Catering and domestic services can be run by an in-house team or by an outside contractor. There are lots of issues affecting the operation with the health of patients being of paramount importance, despite very limited budgets. Hospital staff and visitors also need to be serviced, with different needs from patients who are there for 24 hours a day, often for a long period. Apart from these commercial aspects, the main operations (cleaning and patient feeding) tend to be regarded as cost-only operations.

Education

Catering can range from school meals (often run by a local authority caterer) to residential services in a university. Contract caterers may be employed to run on-site catering in partnership with the college or university management, bringing professional expertise and purchasing power.

Volumes can be enormous – some schools may be serving 1,000 lunches a day and colleges even more. There may be a captive market (for instance in a boarding school) but often caterers are competing with customers bringing their own food from home. Prices tend to be low (sometimes fixed by the establishment) and so cost control is crucial.

Prison catering

Food is an important part of prison life and can be central to morale, and therefore good behaviour. Budgets are very limited but again three meals a day have to be supplied, as well as drinks and snacks. One of the other benefits to prisoners is that they may have the opportunity to work in the kitchens (saving on staffing costs) which develops their skills and helps them gain employment when they are released.

Tour operators

We tend to think of these as always offering accommodation, but packages may also be a day trip to a tourist destination, a theatre-plus-dinner outing or a day at a sporting event. Here the hospitality may be very simple or of a very high standard, such as a day at the races where a champagne lunch is offered.

Package holidays can be just travel and accommodation or may include meals and excursions as well. Although tour operators are more about organisation than unit management they still need to be aware of customer needs, of pricing techniques and the importance of forecasting.

Attractions

These may also be very complex and offer a variety of types of operation – the attraction itself, a shop, café, picnic areas, vending, ice cream stalls and so on. They can be very seasonal – weekends and school holiday times providing the vast majority of their visitors – which means specific problems in staffing and purchasing of goods. Again there may be retail and service elements involved.

Forces catering

Although modernised considerably in recent years there are still separate 'messes' for different ranks, necessitating different standards of service. Budgets are limited despite the catering staff having to provide three meals a day for what may be very physically-active, hungry consumers often in remote locations and in transit between camps.

The importance of control

Before we look at the basics of finance we need to look at why control is important to all types of hospitality business. If the different aspects of the business – revenues, expenses and assets – can be effectively managed, or 'controlled', then we can maximise profit (or in the case of the non-profit sectors, break even or minimise subsidies).

This means that the business is more secure, and so is your job. Better financial results lead to increased wages, job security, company growth and hence better career prospects. Also, your wages mean that you contribute to the local economy by spending in shops and leisure facilities, and the taxes you pay help the country as a whole.

The main aspects of control are listed in Table 1.1.

Table 1.1:
Aspects of control

Planning	Company strategy and policies for the business
Operations	Purchasing
	Receiving, storage and issue
	Preparation (including rooms)
	Selling the product or service
	Receiving payment
Management	Efficient systems
	Physical controls
	Supervision
	Identification of problems and revising of systems

A further important control mechanism is external auditing which is a legal requirement for all large businesses.

All these areas involve people – and people don't always act as efficiently as they should for a variety of reasons (some of which we'll look at in the different chapters). As a result there is potential for:

☐ Wastage due to inefficiency

☐ Theft in some form or another.

In other words, there are *always* control problems, but it is the manager's job to minimise these so as to maximise the profit (or minimise the costs) for the business and hopefully then improve their own salary and career prospects.

The main overall ways that these controls are implemented are through:

☐ Separation of duties

☐ Awareness of systems and people

☐ Measurement

☐ Awareness of risk.

Attitudes to theft

First, think about *your* attitude to theft. Do you see small 'fiddles' as a part of pay? If they are underpaid and overworked then staff may see these as being a legitimate part of their income. What about a manager – do they have the same attitude? And what if it's a high value item that goes missing – is there a cut-off point where theft is acceptable or not?

There's often a 'fine line' between what is a legitimate benefit and what is theft or fraud, and the interpretation can actually vary in different operations. The point is that there is a culture within the business that will either encourage or discourage theft, and this will come from the 'top down'. If you are a large business you may well have stringent rules about what you may or may not do – and all staff from the general manager down may not be able to take anything from the business.

However, if your boss sees it as one of the perks to take food (for instance) away then this will impact on you and your colleagues. If the boss can do it, then why not you? If you are inherently honest (as most people are) then it can be very difficult working in a culture where theft is ignored or worse, actively encouraged. Trust is crucial, but so is stringent action when problems are identified.

Tip!   No one is immune to dismissal for theft. Did you know that Escoffier and Ritz were sacked from the Savoy early last century for £15,000 of fraud?

Attitudes can also vary between countries and cultures. The customers and workforce in hospitality are international and the successful manager needs to recognise that this may mean different attitudes towards both the product and control – what is acceptable in one culture isn't in another.

Types of swindle

There are two main ways of swindling from a business – theft and fraud – and we are covering both in this book.

☐ *Theft* is stealing of physical items (including cash)

☐ *Fraud* is using systems to divert money out of the business.

There's a general opinion that theft is committed by staff and fraud by managers and administrators, but this isn't always the case. It usually depends on opportunity.

Why do people steal?

People steal for lots of reasons but there's usually a combination of:

personal need + opportunity + attitude

Need is often because of financial issues. These can be due to genuine poverty or to self-induced problems such as debt, addiction or a desire for a person to appear richer than they really are.

Opportunity is how easy it is to thieve – which is where you come in. If you can reduce the opportunity then you cut out one of the three motivators.

Attitude is partly due to the ethics of the business (which we mentioned earlier) but also of the individual. Some people aren't honest and will try to steal; others will only steal if tempted or provoked. Attitudes can change if the individual feels let down by the employer – somebody who is over-looked for promotion, bored in their job (so stealing becomes a challenge) or bullied by their boss may well take 'revenge' by trying to steal company property.

Stakeholders

We've talked about the basics of control and why it's important to you, but it's relevant to other people too. These are the 'stakeholders' of the business who may be interested in different things and for different reasons. Here are some of them:

Table 1.2: What stakeholders want

Staff (including you)	Want their wages paid, secure jobs, good working conditions and possibly career prospects
Managers	Want the same and perhaps also an annual bonus related to success
Customers	Want to have their needs satisfied, and more
Suppliers	Want to make sure they will be paid too, and that the business will grow and continue to provide them with a market for their goods and services
Banks and building societies	May have lent money and want to make sure that it (and the interest) will be paid
The Government	Wants its taxes paid (and wants successful businesses to generate more taxes)!
Owners	Want a return on their investment, both now and in the future.

Here's something for you to think about. Who are the stakeholders in your organisation? Are there others than those quoted above (for instance, if you work in a hospital, what about visitors and patients)?

Organisational structures

The final part of this chapter provides an overview of the organisation and illustrates how the different departments fit together. In particular we will concentrate on the financial control (or accounts) department and look at the responsibilities of the different areas. Obviously this will vary in different sectors and also according to the type of accounts they do.

As the most complex type of land-based operation is the leisure hotel (cruise ships can have crew as well but often simplify some of their operations) we'll use that as an example. Figure 1.1 shows a typical management structure for a large property.

Typically the top managers form the 'executive committee' and are responsible for several departments, each with their own managers, supervisors and so on. The general manager will focus more on strategic issues, whereas the operations manager (sometimes called a 'hotel manager') will look after the day-to-day running of the property.

Figure 1.1: Organisation chart of a leisure hotel

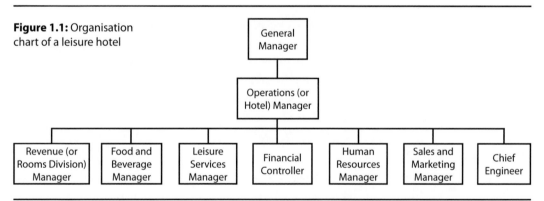

However, structures often relate more to the type of responsibility than the department, so a revenue manager can be responsible not just for rooms but perhaps for food and beverage (F&B) revenue too, in a smaller property. If rooms and F&B are still separate then a revenue manager may look after all room sales – from selling through to check in and out. There may not be a great deal of difference to the traditional rooms division however the focus is very much on maximising revenues. (But does this take the emphasis away from costs? We'll see in later chapters.)

Financial control or accounts department

They look after all the money! This is partly to do with cash but they also maximise revenues and minimise costs by a range of control processes that are divided out among the different sections.

You'll see a large range of job titles and in a big property (around 1,000 rooms) you may find up to 30 people involved in the various areas. It can depend on whether the property has *centralised accounts* or is *self-accounting*.

Centralised accounting

This means that very few of the accounts are prepared at the property and almost all information is transmitted to a head office where it is processed by specialist staff. This approach has grown in recent years with the rapid rise in technology, with easy transmission of data, and is particularly appropriate for fairly simple operations such as lodges and fast-food restaurants.

For instance, when the till system (whatever the sector) is closed down at the end of each day the information on sales, cash received, credit cards and products sold can all be automatically transferred to the main system. When goods are delivered the details are scanned into another computer linked to the main system.

Where centralised systems are used there is little need for a control department because all information is simple and very tightly managed. The management team will then have to perform what's called a 'self-audit' by completing checklists that list a range of procedures daily and periodically, which ensures that checks are taking place. It's also very cheap to operate which means lower costs and hence lower prices for customers.

Self-accounting

Here the local property does all its own accounts – gathers all the revenues, including all debts, pays all invoices, produces final profit and loss and balance sheets and then pays its own taxes. Independent businesses are almost all like this, but so are some large properties that are part of a group, often for tax reasons. This type of property needs a lot of on-site control staff, in the various areas.

Here it's essential that all the responsibilities are segregated so that there's no possibility of fraud – so for instance the person who receives the cheques in the mail doesn't pay them into the bank, and somebody else has to check them off against debtors. This is time-consuming and expensive but essential from an audit perspective.

A variation on this is that you do most of these tasks but a few (such as credit control, payroll, purchasing or reconciliation of taxes) are handled by head office. This is called 'semi-self-accounting'.

Activity	Do you have a control or accounting office – either on-site or at head office? You could talk to the controller and find out what type of accounts they have.

Here's what all the people do in a self-accounting unit:

Financial controller

The manager of the finance or accounts department who is responsible for all the activities as well as the people. In a self-accounting unit she or he may be called a *financial director* and have legal as well as managerial responsibilities. They have to ensure that all controls (*audits*) are performed and that the accounts give a 'true and fair view' of the financial position at the end of each month. They are often formally qualified in accounting.

Assistant controller

Second in command – in a big unit this may be the person who actually manages all the day-to-day business.

Revenue controller (or 'income auditor')

This person checks that all the revenues that have been processed via the various departments are accurate and that everything that has been consumed has been paid for. Sometimes this is done by night audit staff.

Credit controller and sales ledger staff

She or he manages the sales ledger (or 'accounts receivable') which records all the debtors. They approve all requests for credit, check and process invoices, chase customers who don't pay and then process payments. They may also process charge card and company credit card payments.

Purchase ledger (accounts payable)

Checks and pays all the invoices due to suppliers for goods, for services, utilities and to governments.

General cashier

The general cashier checks all the cash that has been received from a variety of sources, banks it and may reconcile all bank statements with the assistant controller. Cash includes cheques, credit cards and foreign exchange. They will also check the various floats in the property or unit with a member of security.

Food and beverage controller

May have equal status with the assistant controller and is responsible for staff in the purchasing and stores area. They check all aspects of food and beverage, from purchasing through delivery, storage and issue to departments. They are also responsible for all the stocktaking (inventory) and hence the calculation of cost of sales.

Computer services or IT department staff

Sometimes these staff report to the controller, others may report to the front office or direct to the GM, with responsibility for all hardware and software. In a smaller operation these responsibilities may be held by the Controller as well and form part of their job description. Many IT systems are located remotely from the business, and may be outsourced to an external provider.

Payroll clerk

Checks all the timesheets (manual or technological) and processes payments to staff. They need to know a lot about the legal aspects of employment – maternity/paternity and sick pay, for instance, can be very complicated. They need to liaise a lot with the human resources department.

Month end

You should now appreciate some of the complexity of the control area and the types of jobs that people do.

Finally, a brief word about 'month end'. This is the period around the last day of the month when all transactions have to be processed up to date, when the stocktaking (inventories) are done, and when lots of additional calculations are processed in order to produce the final accounts. It forms a key part of the overall financial control framework. We'll look a bit more at some of these in the next chapter.

Accounts staff can get a bit stressed at month end as all data has often to be processed to a very tight schedule in order to produce the 'trial balance' (a list of totals of all the account codes) and then draft accounts. These are then checked and the final accounts produced – some companies like to do all this in only two or three days. Managers then review their departmental statements (see Chapter 2) and analyse the results using the ratios that have been calculated on the reports. They will be expected to comment on all variances – good as well as bad – and make suggestions for future action.

Activity   Are all these functions performed in your unit or are some outsourced to another area or company? Payroll, for instance, is often processed outside the company because of the complexity of the laws and, as a result, the need for sophisticated computer software.

Summary

Here we have looked at the basic concept of control – prevention of wastage and theft and why it's important to you. We've also looked at some of the main features of the industry and of the different sectors. There has been a review of the organisation of the business and of the control office, and of the jobs that are required in order to produce accurate results for you and other managers. Many of the techniques you'll practise in this book are relevant to most or all sectors, so hopefully they will be useful to you both now and in the future.

Remember though that you always need to think of the customer first – that's your job as a manager. In this book we're going to show that you can both serve the customer and manage the financial aspects at the same time.

2 Understanding management reports

- Profit & Loss report
- Performance analysis
- The Balance Sheet
- Adjustments to accounts

Introduction

In this chapter we'll look at the main type of report that you will need to help you manage your area better – the *profit and loss report*. For different departments you'll see reports that include not only monetary figures but also percentages for the actual amounts, the amounts that were budgeted, and the difference between them. Later in the chapter we'll see how to use these.

There are also statements used by the general manager – a summary profit and loss (P&L) and then the balance sheet which is important when managing stocks, cash and debtors as well as showing the total value and stability of the business. In order to know how all these accounts are put together we will also examine the activities that need to take place at the end of each month.

So by the end of this chapter you should be able to:

■ Identify different items that appear in a profit and loss report

■ Calculate profits for a simple business

■ Calculate variances and percentages

■ Assemble a balance sheet

■ Calculate accruals, prepayments and depreciation.

Financial reports

Some of this may seem a bit 'dry' but you do need to understand the basics of accounts before you can use the information to help you. So please persevere with the 'theory' and then the next chapter will have more practical applications which will seem more relevant to your job, either now or in the future.

Before we look at the P&L we need to clarify what is meant by 'financial reports'. There are two types produced for a commercial business – generally classified as 'financial accounts' and 'management accounts'.

Financial accounts are produced yearly (and half-yearly) and are formal, official records that have to be submitted for legal reasons to tax and company authorities. For a large company they may also be known as 'published accounts'. There are a lot of rules as to how these are presented and some of these will be covered further in Chapter 10 of this book.

Management accounts are used within the business by the managers to help them be more effective – so they should be designed to suit the manager's needs. They are usually produced every month (or period)

which may be a calendar month (so 12 a year) or four weeks (13 a year). Some businesses also have two four-week months and then a five-week month (so 12 in a year again) although this structure can be a bit awkward to manage.

Now let's look at the main accounting statement that a manager needs – the 'P&L' or profit and loss report. (By the way – you can't get profit *and* loss together, can you? But it's always called this – and always abbreviated to P&L, which is what we will call it too).

Profit & Loss Report

This is a statement of the revenue and expenditure (also called sales and costs – the terms tend to be interchangeable) and one minus the other equals profit or loss. We try to avoid using the word 'income' as in the UK it means what we earn and in the USA can mean net profit.

A department which has sales is called an 'operating department' and is a 'profit centre'. You can also have statements for departments that don't have sales – such as maintenance – that are called 'cost centres'. As we saw in Chapter 1, some businesses such as prison catering may only have costs.

So, what is 'profit'? These definitions come from a variety of sources:

☐ Excess of revenue over expenditure

☐ Excess of sales over related costs

☐ Reward for the entrepreneur (owner).

You can also look at the P&L as being a sharing out of the sales, if you have them. Figure 2.1 is an example where the 'cake' represents the sales and the slices the costs and profit.

Figure 2.1: Costs and profits

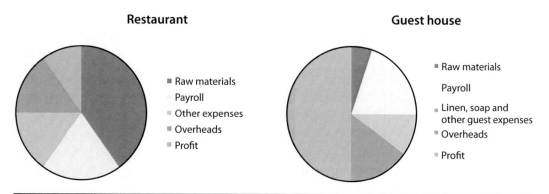

Generally the most profitable type of business is accommodation although the costs of running a building can be high. Profits can be very volatile unless it is part of another business, such as spare bedrooms in a farmhouse run as a B&B. Profitability is relative though – what is good in one sector may be modest in another, and some locations are more profitable than others.

Small businesses

For a simple operation such as a pub, a small restaurant or a bed-and-breakfast you might not need a complicated report – just one that shows you where your money has come from, and gone to. There's no point in wasting time doing extensive accounts if you don't need them (but you *do* need to do some accounts for tax reasons).

For 'Billie's B&B' there isn't a need for complicated accounts – the owners' time is better spent with their customers – so here's the sort of statement that is useful to them:

	£
Sales	20,000
Less cost of sales	(2,000)
Equals gross profit	18,000
Less payroll	(3,900)
Less other controllable expenses	(2,400)
Equals gross operating profit	11,700
Less fixed costs	(5,200)
Equals net profit	6,500

Before we go through line-by-line, a couple of things to tell you. First, you'll see that the figures are laid out in columns. Accounts are always done like this as they are easier for you to read, and it helps the adding and subtracting if this has to be done manually (and spreadsheets, if you use them, are columnar too). The figures are always 'right justified' so that the thousands are always in the same place – again it's easier to read. The titles ('sales' and so on) are left justified although sometimes you may see them indented. For a P&L you don't need to show pence, just round pounds, although when we come to ratios this will change.

Another thing that makes the accounts easier to read is using brackets for minus figures – subtracting is quicker like this than reading a small dash sign. The only problem is that some spreadsheet packages don't have brackets set up automatically so you may need to set this up or show the minus figures in red. Lastly, you underline above a sub-total and below a total so you can see that those are summary figures.

By the way, in Europe all these reports are produced net of Value Added Tax (VAT) which belongs to the government and not the business. In countries with sales and purchases taxes this may be handled differently.

What do all the titles mean?

Revenue (Sales)	All the sales that you make to customers – what they pay for the goods and services they buy from you. They are recorded on the day that the meal is eaten, the room occupied, the flight taken – not on the day that they are actually paid for. We'll talk more about payment in Chapter 7.
Cost of sales (CoS)	The cost of the raw materials used to make the meals and drinks – all the stocks that are used – and also in hotels the cost of telephone units for guest calls and the cost of guest dry cleaning. In retail this may be the cost of goods sold. All other costs such as linen or paper appear elsewhere.
Gross profit (GP)	Sales less cost of sales.
Payroll	All the cost of employing staff – their salaries or wages, overtime and all the benefits associated (also known as 'on cost') such as national insurance, holiday pay, sick pay, uniforms and meals.
Controllable expenses	All other general expenses used in the operation that can be managed and controlled on a daily basis (so paper napkins and electricity but not rent – see below).
Gross operating profit (GOP)	Profit from all items that can be controlled effectively within the unit.
Fixed charges	Rent and rates, depreciation, insurance, loan interest – the 'overheads' of the business. These are the items that can't really be controlled on a day-to-day basis. They are called 'fixed' because they don't change very often – and don't rise and fall with the level of business.
Net profit (NP or NOP)	What you have left.

Note: if you look at an accounting textbook, or see some final accounts for a small business, you may see two further lines – 'less tax' and then 'net profit after tax'. This is tax on profits and we're not covering it in this book as it's very complicated. An accountant is the best person to help you with tax matters as it's a specialist area and errors can be very expensive.

Activity	Do you have a P&L for your unit? Ask to look at it and see how complex or simple it is.

Larger businesses

Most operations, however, are bigger than this with several different areas or departments. A large pub may have two different bars and provide food, a visitor attraction will have a shop and a cafe as well as entrance fees, hospitals need both catering and cleaning services, and so on – so they need more information than shown above.

The managers of these different areas need to know how well or badly their area is performing – and so need their own financial reports. Although you know how many customers you have, and whether they are spending lots of money, you may not always be aware of all the costs associated with this. For instance, if you pay staff overtime it may be far more expensive than hiring in a part-timer for a day. A good manager needs to know everything about the financial aspects as well as the operational ones.

Responsibility accounting

Having your own departmental statement is called 'responsibility accounting' and is linked to a formal structure of departmental statements called the Uniform System of Accounts. The most well-known is the one for hotels ('Lodging', in American terms – abbreviated to USALI – see the Glossary, page 230) but there are other versions for other sectors such as clubs, hospitals and restaurants. Using these means that every unit has the same approach to finance and can be compared against each other (or one business to another) and managers will always understand (in theory!) what appears where.

Departmental statements

The separate statements for each department look a little like Figure 2.2 (they may well be adapted a little to suit different companies).

Figure 2.2: Layout for departmental statements

This month							
Actual	%	Budget	%	Variance	%	Last year	
							Sales
							Cost of sales
							Gross profit
							Payroll
							Expenses
							Departmental profit

What's shown here is only half the statement – on the right-hand side will be a similar set of columns for the 'year to date'. The cost of sales, payroll and expenses are deducted as before.

You can see that there are 'Actual', 'Budget', 'Variance' and 'Last year' columns. The actual is what did happen, the budget indicates what was planned (there's more on this in Chapter 6) and the variance is the difference between them. This variance is always calculated relative to budget so if actual sales were less than budget it would show as a minus. The 'Last year' column shows the previous year's actual figures.

These all allow comparisons to be made between what was expected and what actually happened. For instance, if sales are up then costs should be up too and so should profits. You can look just at money but considering these as a percentage can also help (more on this below).

The rows only show the titles here as well – they would actually include a long list of all the different categories such as types of sales and costs (known as 'account codes' as they all have a separate code number in the accounting system that helps assign them). For instance, if this was used for an attraction's cafe the sales section would show the different types of food such as sandwiches, ice cream, crisps and so on. The expenses will include items like plastic cups and cleaning materials.

If it's a statement for a cost centre then it wouldn't have the first three rows – only the payroll, expenses and departmental cost total.

Activity

Do you have access to a departmental report? If you don't, then ask if you can look at one. Is your statement similar to the example above? You can see the type of headings that appear and the ratios that are calculated. Does this statement actually help you, or the manager of that area, do their job properly, or could improvements be made?

The general manager then receives a statement that consolidates or accumulates all these departmental statements together – this is known as the 'front page P&L'. It's designed to fit on one page so that it can be read easily and so summarises many of the figures – it doesn't include all the detail that your departmental statement would have. Again there's a current month and then a year-to-date set of columns. Figure 2.3 is an example for a hotel.

The top sections summarise all the operating departments followed by the cost centres which service the whole establishment which appear below the DOP (departmental operating profit) line.

Figure 2.3: Layout for 'front page' statements

	Actual		Budget		Variance		Last year	
	£	%	£	%	£	%	£	%
Sales								
Rooms								
Food								
Beverage								
Other								
Total sales								
Gross profits								
Rooms								
Food								
Beverage								
Other								
Total gross profit								
Payroll								
Benefits								
Total payroll								
Expenses – departmental								
Departmental operating profit								
Undistributed operating expenses								
Administration								
Energy								
Repairs & maintenance								
Sales & marketing								
Gross operating profit								
Fixed charges								
Net profit								

Exercise 2.1

Now here's a chance for you to do a small exercise to practise putting the numbers together. This is a pub with rooms, so please do separate departments (even though they are very small) and the front page P&L. Budget figures are included so you can calculate variances as well.

The answers to all exercises are at the end of the book.

	Actual (£)	Budget (£)
Food & beverage sales	12,000	12,500
Cost of sales	3,800	3,800
Accommodation sales	1,900	1,950
Wages – food and beverage	2,700	2,700
Employee benefits – food and beverage	500	500

Wages – accommodation	400	400
Employee benefits – accommodation	80	80
Food and beverage expenses	1,600	1,600
Accommodation expenses	200	200
Administration expenses	1,100	1,100
Rates	500	500
Maintenance costs	100	100
Depreciation	1,400	1,400

Tip It's often easiest to set out all the titles first and then put in the numbers. Lastly you do the addition and subtraction. Another tip is to tick off every number and title that you use from the question when you use them in the answer. You'll then know you haven't forgotten anything.

Performance analysis

Now that we've had time to look at this main statement, what do we *do* with it? What should you, as a manager or supervisor, use these for?

It is the departmental reports that are likely to be of most value to you. You can:

☐ Compare actual to budget, and to last year, in money

☐ Compare these by different percentages

☐ Compare average spends

☐ Look at productivity

☐ Look at costs per customer.

Variances

First you can just look at the variance between actual and budget. Variances can be good as well as bad. but it depends on whose perspective you look from! A high cost of labour may be bad for profits but good for customers, so you do need to find the balance between good service and good cost.

Why don't we just look at variances, though? If you look at the F&B department results for the pub with rooms that we did before, you can see that there's a big variance in money terms between the actual and the budget profits, although the sales show only a small variance. The tendency is just to look at money without seeing where the problem lies. Is it revenue or is it costs? But – if revenues are down then surely costs should be too? If you only look at variances in money amounts then you don't know if the costs are right for this level of revenues.

Now you can compare one percentage to another. You'll see that the budget cost percentage was lower than the actual but that the budget and actual payroll amounts are equal. That means that there's potentially a problem – the cost amount of payroll should have been reduced so that the percentage stays the same. (You can also use this if the actual is higher than budget.)

You'll see that the percentage of profit to sales is worse for the actual than the budget so, although the sales are up, profits haven't risen as much. If you look at the costs percentages you'll see where the problem is (cost of sales). This tells you that you've a problem in that area, which wouldn't have been evident if you'd only looked at the totals.

You can also look at the average amount you get from each customer and the average costs, and see how much profit is generated. (You'll see how to calculate these in later chapters.) If the pub served 1,250 customers then the average spend on F&B would be £9.60.

What's a percentage?

(Just in case you've not done them for a long time.) A percentage is the proportion of one figure relative to another, expressed in parts of 100. So half an apple is 50% of the total and a quarter is 25%. For control purposes we normally add one decimal point (tenths of a percentage) so half is expressed as 50.0% and a third as 33.3%. We'll see how to calculate these a bit further on.

The percentages for the Actual and Budget columns are all expressed relative to sales – so the GP (gross profit) percentage is the proportion of GP in money to the sales figure. The variance percentage for any item is the variance in money as a percentage of the budget.

Tip   Want to check if the percentages are correct? Add them up in the same way as you add the money amounts. So, on the front page, actual column, add 86.3+13.7 = 100, subtract 27.3=72.7 and so on all the way down to the net profit. This is called 'cross casting'.

So, who needs them?

Answer – the stakeholders of the organisation who we discussed in Chapter 1 – management, staff, creditors, owners and so on. They all use ratios to compare one business to another, one unit to another, one month to another. Using ratios means that you can have a 'common size' for comparison, for instance:

☐ Seat turnover in one pizza restaurant to another

☐ Average room rate in a budget hotel compared to last year before they built the extension

☐ Meal cost per person from one hospital to another

☐ Profits from one pub chain to another

☐ Average bet in a casino

☐ Type of customers (called 'market segments' but you could also differentiate by age range).

It doesn't matter if one unit is twice the size of another – by using ratios you can make comparisons.

There are some 'key ratios' for revenue, cost, cash and stocks and productivity areas that we will look at later but you also need to be aware of overall profit (or cost) ratios, which we'll cover briefly now.

'Bottom line' results

At general manager and company level the emphasis is often very much on the 'bottom line'. This is always looked at in money terms but also, depending on the business and the sector, the focus may be on percentages, amount per customer, or both. It may also be the GOP level rather than NOP – for instance a restaurant or hotel operated via management contract or franchise often has to pay a fee based on the achieved GOP. Other operations such as shops or cafes at an airport or in a shopping complex, may pay not a fixed rent but one based on a percentage of sales and occasionally on profits. This encourages operators to be efficient in their control of costs and to optimise sales.

Why not try to calculate the percentages and average spends yourself? You can practise on the pub P&L, above. Then you can do the accommodation area – assume they sold 55 rooms. Lastly do the percentages for the front page P&L.

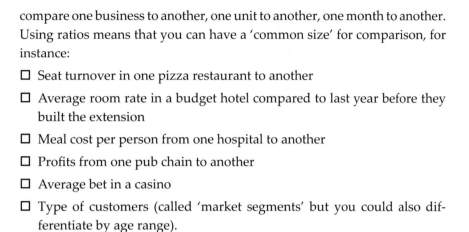

Formula for a cost percentage[1] $= \dfrac{\text{Cost £}}{\text{Sales £}}$ %

Formula for a variance percentage $= \dfrac{\text{Variance £}}{\text{Budget £}}$ %

Formula for an average spend[2] $= \dfrac{\text{Sales £}}{\text{Number of customers (or rooms)}}$

[1](You can use the same approach for a profit %)
[2](This is expressed as £ and pence)

Tip

How to do a percentage:

Type the top figure in the formula into your calculator, hit the divide key, type in the bottom figure then hit the percentage key. This will give you the answer with the decimal point in the right place, so you don't need to bother with multiplying by 100.

For cost centres the percentage is calculated relative to the total sales of the business (so for example energy in a hotel is expressed as a percentage of total hotel sales).

The Balance Sheet

Now we need to look at the second main statement that is used by the unit to help manage the business. These balance sheets may not appear in all operations – if your unit is part of a larger division or company then all these items below may be managed 'higher up'. Even if that is the case, however, it's useful for you to see how your actions in the area say of cash and stocks can affect the value of the business.

The balance sheet (BS) is a statement taken at a specific date (compared to the P&L which accumulated the figures over a period) – so it's often been described as a 'snapshot'. It's a report on the *assets* and *liabilities* of the unit, on the last day of the period. These assets and liabilities can be either long-term (fixed) or short-term (current) in the way they behave.

A bit of accounting theory here – the concept of 'double entry book-keeping' was invented hundreds of years ago by a monk. You don't need to understand how it works, but the basic 'accounting equation' is that:

☐ Everything that is *owned* (an asset) is matched by

☐ Everything that is *owed* (a liability)

And so the total of the *assets* equals the total of the *liabilities*.

Here's some examples you might be familiar with. 'Long term' means that they won't change much in a year whereas short-term ones often change daily. You'll see why they are split a bit later on.

Assets (*we own*)

Fixed assets (lasting more than a year)

☐ Land and buildings
☐ Furniture, fixtures and equipment
☐ Vehicles

Long-term investments

- ☐ Investments (e.g. shares) in other companies
- ☐ Bank and building society (long-term) deposits

Current assets

- ☐ Bank balances (current accounts) and floats
- ☐ Stocks of food, drink and so on
- ☐ Debtors (people who owe us money – in some businesses may be called 'receivables')
- ☐ Prepayments (items paid for in advance – see below)

Liabilities (*we owe*)

Current liabilities

- ☐ Creditors (people we owe money to, may be called 'payables')
- ☐ Accruals (things we have used but not yet paid for – more below)
- ☐ Bank overdraft (if you have one)

Fixed liabilities

- ☐ Long-term loans such as mortgages

Capital

- ☐ Capital (the original investment in the business to start it up. It belongs to the owners so counts as a debt because, if the company were to close down, it should be repaid)
- ☐ Net profit (this is owed to the owners as their reward for the investment they put in)
- ☐ Drawings (money taken out of the business as profits by the owners)

You might have all of these or only some of them. You might just rent your building or equipment rather than own it, for instance, or you may only accept cash payments and so have no debtors.

Exercise 2.2

Decide where some of these items might appear in the balance sheet:

Point of sale system	Mortgage
Delivery van	Phone units used but not paid for
Staff accommodation that is owned	Amount owing from a customer
Stocks of frozen food	Overdraft
Amount owing to a supplier	Yearly rental on coffee machine, paid in advance

Remembering that as *assets = liabilities* you can also see that all assets will also equal capital and other liabilities.

Exercise 2.3

Please can you fill in the gaps so you can see how it works:

	Assets		Capital		Liabilities
	(£)		(£)		(£)
A	2,800	=	[ ]	+	2,100
B	285	=	226	+	[ ]
C	52,000	=	[ ]	+	20,600
D	[ ]	=	3,400	+	1,500

Balance sheet format

Now let's look at the format of the BS. The simple layout is:

	Assets	Liabilities
Fixed	_____	_____
Current	_____	_____
Total	=	

You can re-work the statement so that all the assets, less the current liabilities, will equal the capital and other long-term liabilities. This is the basis for the standard statement that we normally see today.

	Cost	Less depreciation	=	Net value
Fixed assets				
Current assets				
Less current liabilities	_____			
= Working capital				
= Net assets				_____
Financed by				_____
(Long-term liabilities)				_____

Note that the total of the 'Financed by' section always *balances* (equals) with the total net assets. We will cover depreciation later in this chapter. The working capital figure (current assets less current liabilities) shows the amount of money available to run the business on a day-to-day basis. You'll see why this is important when we look at cash and stocks in Chapter 7.

Exercise 2.4

Create a balance sheet using this information and the layout given above:

	(£)
Cash and floats	1,700
Amounts due to suppliers	4,300
Amounts due from customers	500
Profit for the year	1,200
Equipment	22,000
Food stocks	1,150
Owners' capital	27,000

TIP What if it doesn't balance?

1. Tick off all your entries (on the question and on your answer) again to check that they've all been used.

2. Check all your additions and subtractions. If these don't work, see what the difference is between the two figures. Can you see a figure on the BS that is the same? If so (and this isn't likely if you've done the first step) see if you've written it correctly.

3. If you are still out of balance then divide the difference by two. Can you find this new figure anywhere? If so, then you will have added it instead of subtracting, or vice versa – doing this *doubles* the variance.

4. Make the correction and then check the balance again.

5. If you still don't balance then it's likely you've done this adding/ subtracting mistake more than once, so check everything again and you should find the error.

Owners' returns

Lastly, owners will also look at the return on the capital they have invested. There are some very complex calculations you can use which are based on company reports (see Chapter 10) but you can also do a simple calculation which compares the profit to the capital as a percentage. The formula is:

$$\text{Return on investment} = \frac{\text{Profit £}}{\text{Capital invested}} \%$$

Adjustments to Accounts

Cost of Sales

First, an adjustment you are probably familiar with. Most hospitality businesses have stocks of one sort or another and the value of this (particularly if it's alcohol) can be very high. You don't want to show all this as sold the moment you've purchased it as this would distort your figures and accounts have to show the cost of the items used to make the sales. So you need to ensure that the value of the items you haven't sold (stock) is shown on the BS and not on the P&L.

First you need to physically count the stocks (see Chapter 7) and then the value is used for the closing stock figure on the BS. In order to calculate the cost of sales – the amount used by customers – you need to use this formula:

Opening stock (your closing stock at the end of last month is the opening for this)
+ Purchases and delivery charges, etc.
= Total stock available
− Cost of staff meals (even if off the customer menu)
− Value of the closing stock
= What you have used to serve customers (cost of sales).

An example:

	(£)
Opening stock (as at the start of the period)	10,000
+ purchases	65,000
=	75,000
− cost of staff meals	(5,000)
− closing stock	(12,000)
= Cost of sales	58,000

Exercise 2.5

Here's one to try: Opening stock £490, purchases £11,060, closing stock £530 and staff meals £920

Activity

Do you have Cost of Sales (CoS)? Who calculates it? Are there any other additions or subtractions that have to be made before it can be finalised?

Prepayments

Some items have to be purchased in advance – for instance: annual rental or maintenance contracts. Here you don't want the whole amount to 'hit' your P&L all at one time as this will distort your profits. Instead they are *amortised* or split out for the months they refer to. It's classed as a current asset because technically we own it as it's been paid for.

	(£)
Contract (per year)	24,000
Charge per month	2,000
End April 2 months used	4,000
10 months outstanding (prepayment)	20,000

The prepaid amount stays on the BS, reducing each month when the charge goes to the P&L.

Exercise 2.6

Rental on equipment per year £10,400. How much is the prepayment per period if there are 13 periods per year?

If the invoice is paid in January (the first period of the financial year) and now is the eighth period, how much has been amortised (used) and how much remains on the BS?

Accruals

For the current liabilities an accrual is the opposite of a prepayment – it's an estimate for the cost of something that has been used but not yet paid for. At the end of each month it's unlikely that you will have been billed for everything so there tends to be a few days worth of, for instance, electricity, that has been used but not charged for. You may also have not been billed for food or drink delivered on the last day of the month. It's a current liability because it's owed to suppliers although hasn't yet been invoiced (creditors are those that have invoiced you and are ready to be paid).

	(£)
Electricity bill to 12 September (28 days' worth)	560
Approximate daily usage	20
Accrue 18 days	360

There would be a charge to the electricity code on the P&L as a cost and to the accruals on the BS (that double-entry approach again).

Activity Can you think of any more examples of items needing to be accrued in your area?

Depreciation

The most complex month-end adjustment is usually for depreciation. First we need to look at the fixed assets category again. You'll have seen that these are items that are likely to last more than a year and are high in original cost. Again it would be too expensive for them to be charged totally to the P&L when bought (though different companies have different rules on this).

You need to estimate how long they will last before they need replacement, and charge out a proportion of the cost each month. The main method is called 'straight line depreciation' and assumes that the items lose value at the same pace each month and year. Figure 2.4 shows what the value would look like.

Figure 2.4: Straight line depreciation

Item costing £5,000 depreciated over 5 years so value divided into 5 equal parts				
£1,000	£1,000	£1,000	£1,000	£1,000
Year 1	Year 2	Year 3	Year 4	Year 5

Hence the same amount is charged out each year, divided equally per month.

Here's an example: Cost £12,000, estimated lifespan is 5 years (normally expressed as 20%) so the depreciation is £200 per month or £2,400 a year.

	(£)
Purchase	12,000
Depreciation Year 1	(2,400)
Balance at end Year 1	9,600
Depreciation Year 2	(2,400)
Balance at end Year 2	7,200
Depreciation Year 3	(2,400)
Balance at end Year 3	4,800
Depreciation Year 4	(2,400)
Balance at end Year 4	2,400
Depreciation Year 5	(2,400)
Balance at end Year 5	0

The charge is subtracted from the fixed assets on the BS and then appears as a fixed charge on the bottom of the P&L, after the GOP line as it isn't controllable.

Reducing balance and valuation are two other methods that are not used very much now so we won't bother with them.

Exercise 2.7

Here's a depreciation calculation for you to do:

Equipment £6,800, depreciated at 10% per annum (= 10 years' life)

Furniture £2,600, depreciated at 20% per annum (= 5 years' life)

Exercise 2.8: Rural restaurant

Now let's try and do everything so far. This exercise needs you to calculate depreciation and so on, prepare a P&L and then the BS. Note that the Net profit from the P&L goes to the BS and is added to last year's profit to date to give a cumulative profit. You could also calculate some percentages.

Tip   Do the workings out first – for prepayments, accruals, cost of sales and depreciation. This makes it easier to put together the P&L and BS.

The accounts list the following balances for the year ending December. You are asked to prepare the P&L and balance sheet.

	(£)		(£)
Floats	60	Repairs and maintenance	1,275
Drawings *(see note below)*	3,000	Equipment	10,200
Sales	39,852	Furniture	3,900
Creditors	2,520	Payroll	8,835
Owners' capital	33,510	Stock as at previous year	738
Rates	870	China, glass & silver stock	1,500
Utilities	1,395	Laundry	1,239
Marketing	300	Miscellaneous expenses	3,528
Purchases	16,482	Debtors	1,560
Buildings	18,000	Cash at bank	3,000

The following transactions have not yet been processed.

	(£)		(£)
Stock at the end of this year	804	Accrual for utilities unpaid	342
Prepayment on rates	174	Accrual for wages unpaid	90
Marketing prepaid	60	Staff meals	£1,380

Depreciate equipment at 10% p.a.; furniture at 15% p.a.

Note   **Drawings** is money that has been taken out of the business by the owner (a sole proprietor – see Chapter 10). They don't pay tax on it as part of the business, but once it becomes their property then they would have to pay personal income tax on it.

Summary

In this chapter we've looked at the two principal reports that are used to help in the management of the hospitality business – the profit and loss and balance sheet reports. We have also reviewed the various activities and adjustments that need to take place in order for the month-end accounts to be assembled in order to present a 'true and fair view' of the business. You have:

■ Reviewed the structure of the P&L report including the standard format known as the Uniform System

■ Considered the basic principles pertaining to the balance sheet and reviewed the layout in current common usage

■ Practised calculating accruals, prepayments and depreciation

■ Learned of the need for a format that shows 'common size' to allow comparisons

■ Practised some common ratios.

3 Managing revenue

- Features of different areas
- Identifying areas for action
- Stakeholders
- Improving revenues
- Improving sales

Introduction

Maximising revenues is as important as minimising costs to achieve profits. The usual (sales and marketing or revenue management) approach is to try and gain additional business – and we will cover some of this here. However, since this is a book about control we'll be looking more at ways of ensuring that you get all your revenue from existing customers.

If you work in a section where only costs occur, much of this chapter may seem irrelevant, but you may have 'revenue' from a subsidy or allowance and you certainly still have customers. I hope you will gain an insight into practices in other sectors that may help you in the future, if not just now.

You have to ensure that everything a customer consumes is actually paid for and that you aren't giving it away, wasting it or losing it to fraud. This applies to a take-away, a drink, a package holiday or a five-star meal – all can lose revenues by inadequate control. In some sectors this may be more obvious as they have much stronger control mechanisms – in others it may be difficult to see easily where problems might occur.

We look at pricing in Chapter 5 but it's important to recognise now that there shouldn't be a conflict between marketing and control – the stakeholder approach means that everybody is interested in the business doing well. The controller wants good revenues as well as the marketing or revenue manager because this should result in good profits, which means good employment for them (in all its aspects).

By the end of this chapter you should be able to:

- Identify the features which may impact on revenue maximisation
- Understand the differences between revenue management and revenue control
- Identify where shortfalls can occur, using ratios
- Calculate ratios for a range of revenue areas
- Utilise methods of improving revenues.

Features of different sectors

Before we look at some general areas of controlling revenue let's look at some more features of the hospitality industry that might influence revenue patterns and hence control processes. Many of these features are common to several hospitality sectors, to a greater or smaller extent.

Nature of the product

The product may be very complex (leisure hotels, cruise lines, theme parks) or very simple. A guesthouse may offer room and breakfast only, with no restaurant, room service, bar or other facilities. A fish-and-chip shop may sell only eight or 10 items, being more interested in concentrating on speed of service than the range of products.

One single purchase may have several elements – a take-away order could include a dozen things and so can a package holiday. All these elements can be different in behaviour and so need controlling in different ways.

Even within a single identifiable product you may have lots of different prices available – a business class hotel may sell a standard single room at 10 different rates to separate types of customer, from the quoted 'rack rate' to a heavily discounted one for a favoured client at a quiet period. A double measure of gin may be priced differently if sold during a 'happy hour', in a cocktail or as a standard product – and differently again if in a mini-bar. Airline, rail tickets and accommodation can be discounted at different rates depending on how far in advance you buy them. Pricing at different levels is covered in Chapter 5.

Seasonality

Some businesses and sectors have distinct peaks and troughs in trade and 'seasonality' causes natural rises and falls independent of one-off economic changes. Seasonality is mainly used to mean different times of the year but you also get changes from day to day. Examples of seasonality are:

☐ The 'banquet season' before Christmas when the majority of functions are held

☐ Resorts may be strongly dependent on the weather

☐ Attractions are noticeably busier in school holidays and at weekends

☐ Soup bars and hot food counters may be far busier in cold wet weather than on warm summer days.

Mixed markets

Some sectors have very strongly defined markets whereas others such as fast food appeal to a much wider range of customers. Contract caterers may offer different types of meal to the same group of employees – a main cafeteria, a deli-bar and hospitality suites. Individual guests may change their market type – for instance they will spend a lot of money on a meal if on company business (say £100 per person if they're not paying!) but if they take their family for a meal (with their own money) then a spend of £15–20 each is more likely.

One business may have one type of market at one time and a different type at another. Restaurants offer fixed-price menus at lunchtime to attract office workers but in the evening have an à la carte menu to attract a different type of customer who will stay a lot longer and spend more money. Levels of trade in pubs vary dramatically with the time of day and day of the week. Another example would be a leisure club that takes groups of schoolchildren during weekdays but individuals in the evenings and at weekends.

All these form *market segments*, a term usually used in hotels to describe the different types of customers. Here you may get 'rack rate' (full rate) guests, business, tour groups, leisure, conference, airline crew and so on – a big hotel may have more than 17 different segments during a week.

A hospital may have patients, visitors and staff and a university have residential and commercial customers, students and staff. The occupancy statistics will include the split into segments as well as the overall result. Theme parks can split into age groups according to ticket type so that they can target their advertising to the right groups at the right time.

Activity   It's always useful to be able to identify where your customers come from. This helps you target your marketing differently to suit the different needs. Think about the customers where you work. Can you split them into 'market segments'?

Captive markets

These occur for such customers as factory workers or hospital staff (as well as patients, army employees or prisoners) and may seem to automatically generate revenue but there's a real danger that the customers can easily get 'menu fatigue'. This has the effect that they might start to bring their own sandwiches, or sneak out to the pub at lunchtime, so there's an employment as well as a feeding issue here.

Competition

Another issue can be competition for supply. A 'competitor analysis' is normally used to find the direct competition for your business (other restaurants, pubs and so on) but you could also use it on a smaller scale to see if there is any other type of competition. For a pub this could be not just other pubs and wine bars but people going to the off-licence and taking beer or wine home for a 'night in'. Supermarkets are competition for restaurants with their ranges of ready meals and you may buy or rent a DVD (to go with those beers) instead of going to the cinema.

Another example seen recently has been the impact of WiFi on hotel internet charges. Guests used to expect to pay an additional charge for internet access, but with widespread wireless networking many now have to offer this 'free' with a consequent loss of revenue to the hotel.

| Activity | Think about how a supermarket sells its products to different target markets. Loyalty schemes aren't just to persuade you to buy by giving you points – they are also designed to find out lots about your spending patterns and target you 'individually' as a customer. |

Identifying areas for action

There are two main ways of identifying areas that you need to address – Ratios and 'management by walking about' (MBWA).

MBWA

Nothing can beat the effectiveness of an alert manager's eye, both for seeing problems (and hopefully good things too) and for ensuring that correct actions are taken. If a manager or supervisor is seen to be watching what happens, and reacts to it, then the staff will also be alert. Taking action means praising the good things and highlighting those that need improvement. If there is a problem then you can discuss changing the approach, retrain staff or add new checks as needed. By 'leading from the top' your staff will strive harder for perfection too.

Some people steal or are wasteful if they have the opportunity, and watching what they are doing reduces this. If you show that you don't approve of it, they are less likely to steal as well. By maintaining staff morale and ensuring that they are treated fairly you will improve attitudes to control. You may not be able to influence pay levels (poor pay is another reason for theft) but you can reward staff in other ways (praise, nomination for Associate of the Month, telling senior management, and so on). Showing you care matters in more ways than one.

> **Mini-case**
>
> A member of staff suddenly started making mistakes with a consequent loss in his bar takings. He'd always been an excellent employee but now there were clear grounds for disciplinary action. The manager noticed that the barman looked haggard and unwell. It emerged that he and his family had been mugged in their own home the previous week and as a result he wasn't sleeping well. They gave him some (paid) time off and two weeks later he returned, back to his old efficient self again.

Using ratios

We looked at the general reasons for using ratios in the previous chapter. As a manager or supervisor you can't see everything so using ratios can identify areas for concern so you can then target your actions. If you work in a hotel front office area you won't be able to work 24 hours a day and the night staff check in guests too. By using occupancy and housekeeping reports you can make sure that all rooms occupied have been charged for. If the average spend achieved per customer falls (in any type of unit) then you know you've got a problem with customers either not being charged for everything or staff pocketing the takings. You can identify control problems and also opportunities for increasing revenues through marketing and selling.

Performance for revenue areas is measured by:

☐ Variance analysis, comparing actual to budget, as we did in Chapter 2

☐ Daily, weekly and monthly sales

☐ Occupancy

☐ Average spend per customer, by different types

☐ Sales mix

☐ Profitability percentages.

Here are some of the key ratios that are used in the business to show how effective management is at controlling revenue. The formula for calculating them is shown and then a brief explanation of how they are used. There appear to be a lot of them but they can really be divided into just a few types – those that look at the number of customers, those that look at how much they spend and then the comparisons between revenue types.

Once you have learned one type of ratio you can use it for different sectors – so although you will see occupancy ratios separately for F&B and rooms they are really very similar both in calculation and in meaning.

Volume

Let's review the ratios that look at volumes first – often known as 'occupancy'. These take the number of customers you achieve divided by the capacity. In hotels the capacity is rooms available, in restaurants it is seats available and in exhibition centres it's space for stands. You can also use this for golf lessons, therapy sessions, car parking spaces and many more.

This ratio looks at rooms sold as a proportion of rooms available. It gives you a measure of how efficient you are at selling the space you had available on the day. You could also use it for cabins sold on cruise ships or for long-stay hostels or apartments. You would normally do this calculation once per day and then for the month and the year. It's unlikely that you would achieve over 100% occupancy in a day unless you have a lot of day-lets (say to airline crews) and very efficient housekeeping staff.

$$\text{Room occupancy \%} = \frac{\text{Rooms sold}}{\text{Rooms available}} \%$$

Your customers may also be split into market segments – yes, you can split by segment and type although this is only worthwhile if your volumes are high enough. So there's no point in splitting too much if you only have 100 customers a day, but if you have 1,000 or 10,000 then it's definitely helpful.

Tip   Remember decimal points on percentages – always show at least one, e.g. 50.3% not 50%.

Some accommodation sectors also look at the number of beds occupied. You can calculate this either by doing the bed occupancy (beds sold divided by beds available) or by finding the number of double rooms sold as a proportion of the total. This result may be a bit distorted if you then have triple rooms or quadruples.

$$\text{Double occupancy} = \frac{\text{Double rooms sold}}{\text{Total rooms sold}} \%$$

The same type of ratio can be used in food and beverage outlets. Occupancy of seats is shown as a percentage, whereas other businesses may want to know how many times a seat is 'turned'. This uses the number of customers ('covers') divided by the seats you have available. For a small restaurant with a single sitting occupancy may be less than 100 per cent (a full house may be unusual) but for a staff cafeteria each seat may be occupied several times in a day, so an occupancy of several hundred per cent (or a seat being turned many times) is usual.

$$\text{Seat occupancy \%} = \frac{\text{Seats sold}}{\text{Seats available (this could be per hour if high turnover)}} \%$$

The following examples show similar types of ratio. All these are really the same type – they show the average volume of customers over a period. This is useful as an overall guide and for comparing to budget or to last year but for use in planning (see the chapter on forecasting) you really need to plot these on a daily or an hourly basis to see the peaks and troughs in the business. Casinos use two similar ratios – 'Average time played' (at a table or on a slot machine) and 'Decisions per hour' – which means the number of bets that are made for the time that they play.

$$\text{Average customers per day} = \frac{\text{Total customers per month}}{\text{Number of days in period/month}}$$

$$\text{Customers per hour} = \frac{\text{Total customers}}{\text{Number of hours in day}}$$

$$\text{Passengers per flight} = \frac{\text{Total passengers}}{\text{Number of flights}}$$

$$\text{Visitors per day} = \frac{\text{Total visitors}}{\text{Number of days in period/month}}$$

$$\text{Average covers per meal period[1]} = \frac{\text{Covers sold}}{\text{Number of meals in period}}$$

[1]Can be done for separate meals – breakfast, lunch, dinner

Are there any others you can think of?

Spends per customer

Now let's look at how much they spend. We'll mainly look at revenue but also consider profit. You'll notice that the results are given in pounds and pence – as mentioned in Chapter 2, this is always done with ratios so it is £10.16 not £10.

Average room rate

(hotels, hostels, residential, cruises) $= \dfrac{\text{Rooms revenue}}{\text{Rooms sold}}$ £p

Spend per customer

(Cover, guest, visitor, traveller, shop purchaser,etc) $= \dfrac{\text{Revenue}}{\text{Customers}}$ £p

Average bet (casino) $= \dfrac{\text{Total betting revenue}}{\text{Customers}}$ £p

The total revenue is divided by the number of customers – whatever they are called (guests, patients, covers and so on). You can do this for overall revenue for the period but it has more value if split into different categories such as food, beverage, retail, entrance fees, beauty therapy – the list is endless. This really helps you see where the sales are coming from, and can then be matched with costs (see next chapter). You can identify which areas are more popular than others, and then consider re-vitalising those that are performing badly.

As with occupancy, you can also split revenue into the market segments to give average spend for different types of customer and into trading periods.

You can also consider the revenue generated by the space available:

$$\text{Room hire per square metre (by day or month)} = \frac{\text{Room hire revenue £}}{\text{Number of square metres of space}} \quad \text{£p}$$

$$\text{Retail revenue per square metre (by day or month)} = \frac{\text{Retail revenue £}}{\text{Number of square metres of retail space}} \quad \text{£p}$$

A further ratio that is used in hotels is revenue per available room (REVPAR) – the average revenue gained from all the rooms you had available (not those actually sold). This is shown in pounds and pence and is used extensively to compare one hotel against another, as published in comparisons of operating statistics (see the reading list).

$$\text{REVPAR – Revenue per available room (per day)} = \frac{\text{Rooms revenue £}}{\text{Rooms available}} \quad \text{£p}$$

Lastly there is yield, which is a measure of efficiency of both average occupancy and average room rate. This ratio takes the REVPAR figure and compares it to the optimum average rate – usually the 'rack' (or published) rate – as a percentage. This shows you how efficient you are in selling both rate and rooms.

$$\text{Yield} = \frac{\text{REVPAR £}}{\text{Potential average room rate £}} \quad \%$$

Another would be REVPASH – Revenue Per Available Seat Hour. Can you think of any others you might use in different types of business?

Profit ratios

The final ratios in this section are to do with profits and you can calculate these for any type of customer as well as show them as a percentage.

$$\text{Profit per customer} = \frac{\text{Net profit £}}{\text{Number of Customers}} \quad \text{£p}$$

$$\text{Profit per staff member *} = \frac{\text{Net profit £}}{\text{Number of Staff}} \quad \text{£p}$$

$$\text{Net profit \%} = \frac{\text{Net profit £}}{\text{Sales}} \quad \%$$

* You could also calculate sales per staff member, especially if they earn bonuses or commission on sales.

Exercise 3.1

Here's an example for you to do – you'll find the answer, as usual, at the end of the book:

		Occupancy (%)
Rooms available	90	
Rooms sold		
Rack rate	5	
Leisure	10	
Business	60	
Total		

Rooms revenue	Total	Average room rate (£)
Rack rate	£550	
Leisure	£650	
Business	£6,000	
Total		

Tip The overall average room rate isn't the average of the three room rates – it's the total rooms revenue divided by the total rooms sold. Try both ways if you wish and see the difference.

Sales mix

Finally you can look at the proportion of individual sales to total sales, and express it as a percentage. The usual split is by type of revenue (food and beverage, retail and entrance fees, for instance) but you can split by meal or trading period. This shows you how much money is being taken at particular times of day or from different sources and again is really useful when it comes to planning for the future. This split will affect the costs too.

$$\text{Food} = \frac{\text{Food sales £}}{\text{Total F\&B sales £}}\ \%$$

$$\text{Retail sales} = \frac{\text{Retail sales £}}{\text{Total sales £}}\ \%$$

$$\text{Breakfast sales} = \frac{\text{Breakfast sales £}}{\text{Total cafe sales £}}\ \%$$

Here's a very simple example:

	(£)	(%)
Room sales	14,000	70.0
Food sales	4,000	20.0
Beverage sales	2,000	10.0
Total sales	20,000	100.0

Activity	Can you think of any more ratios? Consider your area (or one that you know) and see what type of revenue ratios are calculated. Are there any more that could be done but aren't? What ratios might a cruise ship use, for instance?

Improving revenue controls

Now let's review ways of improving revenues. Some are marketing ideas but others are more to do with control – and both are considered in terms of improving efficiency without increasing workload (too much). Revenue control is concerned with ensuring that everything you sell is paid for, whereas revenue management is more about increasing average spends and occupancies.

Some areas have few problems in collecting revenue – no money equals no ticket, for instance. Effective systems (physical, administrative and technological) are crucial in helping maximise revenues (and in minimising costs, of course). Once installed, they should enable you to limit your audit processes to spot-checking where necessary, without having to cross-check every transaction.

First, we'll look at the revenue control aspects, starting with systems, and then move on to consider issues for the particular sectors.

Till systems

In brief, electronic point of sale systems (EPOS) range from quite simple to very sophisticated mini computers – the more you spend, the more control and information you get. Ideally as well as pre-set menu keys you also need a full menu-mix analysis which tells you not only how many you have sold but the cost and selling price of every item. This is really useful as you can see the revenue that you should have taken for the items that have been sold, and can take action if the figures don't match. Many will track staff hours, stock levels and loyalty schemes for you by collating 'points' earned by your customers which can then be exchanged for free or discounted drinks or meals.

Hand-held EPOS systems are now commonly used by waiting staff to take orders that are then transmitted directly to the kitchen (and the customer's bill) without the waiting staff having to leave the customer. This can improve service speed enormously, especially if the kitchen and restaurant are a long way apart.

Property-wide systems

Property management systems (PMS) are very sophisticated computerised systems that run a whole series of functions, usually in a hotel. These usually integrate into other systems such as revenue management, EPOS and all aspects of the main back office accounting system, as well as linking to head office systems.

Losses also occur from either under-ringing or incorrect pricing, so it's crucial to ensure that your billing system is up to date and that there are controls in place to stop errors. If you don't have an EPOS or PMS then you need to ensure that all items consumed are paid for. This means meals, drinks, rooms, rides, beauty treatments and rounds of golf.

Control processes for different sectors

Restaurants

The traditional method of taking an order in restaurants and cafés is to write a guest-check in duplicate for the food with one copy going to the kitchen for the food to be cooked. The other copy stays by the till for the guest bill. These guest checks are numbered so they can be tracked and not re-used. You need to then make sure that the bill is paid, of which more in Chapter 7. If you are using a manual system then it's important to spot-check all these guest checks to see whether every order was served and paid for and that all have been used for what was intended.

For self-service restaurants you either need to have a till at the end of the counter or to be very vigilant to ensure that customers don't walk in – and then eat and walk out without paying. Breakfast in hotels can be a particular issue if you don't check off all room numbers as guests enter the restaurant. The location of the tills does help with maximising the collection of revenue and so, in a food court where there are lots of counters (and hence it looks like a buffet), the tills should be situated so customers are funnelled through them to the seating areas.

Mini-case

A family were staying in a hotel and invited friends to dinner. The restaurant operated a carvery-style operation whereby guests ordered their starter and then chose their own main course. The restaurant manager took their order, noted their room number and that there were two extra covers to be charged. When they checked out at the end of their stay they found that the two extra had not been charged for – a potential loss of £39.

Pubs and bars

In bars and pubs the routine is normally for the customer to order and then give cash in exchange for the drink – which in theory maximises revenue immediately. EPOS systems help ensure customers are charged the correct prices so that there is less opportunity for staff to overcharge and pocket the excess. Drinking is part of the culture and any drinks for staff must be correctly accounted for, whether paid for by customers or by the establishment.

Many establishments allow customers to pay for drinks by credit card, providing that an on-going record is kept so that the customer pays for all the correct items consumed. It's worth having the guest sign for each round separately – if they have too many then they may be incapable of signing the check by the time the bill is presented.

Subsidised and full-cost catering

The subsidy (whether part or total) is often based on the number of customers you serve whether for hospital patients, employee feeding or army trainees. In order to achieve the maximum subsidy you need to ensure that all your customers are counted, and that your number served matches with the figure produced by the organisation paying for it.

This might mean a cross-check between patients registered for treatment and number of lunches served, or staff signing for meals with hours-worked records. Again there's an element of trust but this time between contractor and contractee, so it's important that you maintain that by being as accurate as possible. Even if you have been paid in advance for these customers you still need to ensure that your records are accurate so that you can ensure your cost percentages (see next chapter) are kept in line.

Conference and banqueting and event catering

These operate with very high numbers and often a tight turn-round on meal times, so ensuring that you have recorded all the guests is crucial. The process starts early. Contracts (such as a banquet event order) must be signed off by the organiser for groups, banquets, conferences and so on so that there are no disputes later. This type of agreement means there should be no confusion for anybody, from the head of the company holding the function to the banqueting porter who has to move all the tables around. Again, it's about maximising revenue by minimising potential problems.

Once the guests actually sit down to eat you can check the number against those booked and the meals delivered from the kitchen. This can be almost impossible with a stand-up buffet!

Managing revenue

Complimentary meals

Complimentary can mean a meal given as compensation for bad service (hopefully rare) or for a different business reason such as delays in check-in at a hotel or airport. In restaurants and catering managers and staff may eat 'comps' as part of training – tasting a new menu, for instance. A major part of the food and accommodation offered in casinos may be 'comped' in order to encourage 'high rollers' to spend more money at the tables or on the machines.

Different companies have different attitudes to 'comps' – some account for it all at cost (and adjust the cost of sales figure), others record all at revenue which then shows the true number of customers served. What you need to ensure is that these are properly recorded and justified, and that you are consistent in your approach.

Rooms controls

Staff taking reservations must ensure that all data is correct including billing and rates to be charged. Rooms-sold data is checked against housekeeping reports to ensure that all rooms occupied have been accounted for (paid for or for staff use). The difficulty is in ensuring that the rates charged are not discounted for friends or in return for personal reward. Chance guests, particularly late at night, may offer cash to pay for their room on check-in and it can be tempting for staff to pocket the cash rather than pay it in. Hence the need to cross-check the rooms occupied with the housekeeping report the next morning.

Mini-case

A family booked a specific room at a hotel. When they checked in, they were allocated to a different room that was much smaller and had fewer facilities, although at a lower room rate (£97). They complained and the receptionist moved them to the room they had originally booked.

On check out they found they had only been charged the £97 rate – a potential loss to the hotel of £90 over the three nights. The receptionist had not changed the rate when they moved to the correct room. Yes – it was the same family who had the carvery meal, on the same stay – and they'd been undercharged on previous visits too.

What does this say about the management's (and company's) attitude to control?

Complimentary rooms

Comps are relevant for rooms too. The courier of a tour group is also normally 'comped' so this needs to be carefully costed into the package price you are offering – it isn't really 'free'. Again different companies use different approaches. Usually the cost of the meal or accommodation has already been budgeted for against a cost code and so is charged there – these shouldn't be set against revenue or it will give an inaccurate picture of volumes and spends.

Mini-case

An international hotel group had recently opened its first hotel in London. It seemed like the entire senior management of the company decided it was essential to pay a site visit and asked for complimentary accommodation. The GM (General Manager) complained that this was affecting his revenue, as he couldn't sell to 'paying punters'. Head office agreed and insisted that everybody paid full ('rack') rate so that occupancy and average spend were maintained and the figures not distorted. Surprisingly, once they were asked to pay, demand from these senior personnel declined!

Revenue management

This used to be called yield management and is an approach used in hotels (and also airlines, sports stadia, car hire, cinema tickets, beauty sessions...) that boosts both rate and occupancy. The basic approach is to try to persuade people to stay at the times that you are quieter, to boost both occupancy and average spend. If they want to stay at a premium period then a premium price is charged, such as for package holidays during school holiday periods. Off-peak prices on trains are infinitely cheaper than peak prices to encourage people to travel more. An example for a rail ticket to London:

07.00	Commuters	Price £57
08.15	Late commuters, some leisure travellers	Price £32
09.30	Leisure travellers, with discount card	Price £18

So by travelling two-and-a-half hours later you can save two-thirds of the price – for the same type of seat on the same type of train, for the same journey.

Revenue management is increasingly important for hotels, because once efficient cost controls are in place the only real opportunities for improving profits are in the revenue-generating areas. Figure 3.1 shows a typical occupancy pattern for a hotel for a week.

Figure 3.1: Hotel weekly occupancy pattern

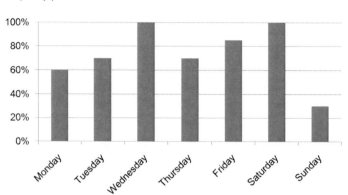

You'll see from the figure that you have very high demand for Wednesday and Saturday, but the days on either side – 'shoulder days' – are less popular. One of the objectives of revenue management is to optimise occupancy on these shoulder days, and to optimise average room rate throughout. One way the business may do this is to impose a 'minimum length of stay' requirement for the Wednesday – so you only take a booking for that night if the customer will arrive on the Tuesday and stay for 3 nights. If demand is exceptional you may also raise prices and close bookings to all but very favoured clients.

Traditionally rates were fixed in advance, and discounts only offered at a late stage if a low occupancy was forecasted. Now, the customer can obtain a discounted rate by booking (and paying) many days in advance of arrival. The closer to the date of arrival that the booking is made, the higher the rate that is quoted.

The critical issue for effective revenue management is accurate forecasting, which require both skilled staff and sophisticated technology (see Chapter 6). Complex spreadsheets and specialist systems are required that analyse past data to enable accurate predictions of future trends. This then gives revenue managers the data they need to make decisions about future bookings – for rates to be quoted, length of stay restrictions, distribution channels and availability to different market segments. Knowledge of the contribution gained from each type of booking allows optimisation of profits as well as revenues.

Given the rate of change with technology, revenue management is a new and dynamic discipline that is being improved all the time. If you want to learn more about it then please read current industry articles, usually via the Internet rather than traditional sources.

Improving sales generally

However, there are other ways that you can improve revenues without using sophisticated systems – such as marketing and up-selling. Here are a range of ideas that are found in most marketing books, so apologies if you've seen them all before. There are a few comments added about the financial implications – which aren't always mentioned by marketers.

You can improve sales either by selling more to your existing customers, or by increasing the number of customers overall. First you need to use ratios to see where the opportunities are – there's no point in trying to increase customers if you don't have the capacity, enough staff or the right equipment.

Increasing spends

Training and incentives

Trained staff are crucial in explaining dishes (or other products for sale), persuading customers to buy (up-selling), serving correct portions, collecting payment and generally keeping customers happy – whatever the type of operation. Happy customers spend more (and tip better)!

Incentive schemes for staff can be very good in persuading them to up-sell to customers, and can help in staff morale, which is likely to mean fewer problems with theft and wastage. Awareness of the impacts on profits helps staff identify where to focus their energies – it's better to promote items with a higher GP – so try and sell a pot of tea rather than an orange juice. It is called menu engineering and is a technique for persuading people to consume different things that will generate more profit, or perhaps are easier to process (and hence less resource-intensive).

Diversification of sale items

This means adding more items for sale that customers will buy as extras to their main product. If you have a teashop you could add a few postcards, pots of jam or craft items – they would look attractive on display (saving the cost of display china, for instance) and could give you extra revenue. A sandwich bar can sell coffee as well as soft drinks and a package holiday offer optional city tours. Some hotels or restaurants display original pictures by local artists on their walls – these save on the cost of buying your own, support local enterprise and can give you commission on every one sold.

You do need to make sure the revenue is kept separate from your own, though, so that there is no dispute at a later stage, either with the supplier or the tax inspector.

Activity

Think of somewhere you visit as a customer (even your local swimming pool). Do they have other products on sale? Could they diversify and offer additional products or service that would add value to your visit and revenue for themselves.

Now think if there is anything your own business could do to add revenue by adding new products or services.

Increasing customers

First of all you need to ensure that you have the capacity to cope with an increase (enough space, staff, equipment, materials and so on). You then need to forecast (see Chapter 6) where your peaks and troughs will be. At peak times you probably have enough business to cope with, but you should be able to identify troughs that you could try to fill.

Activity

Look at your customer flows (do you have an EPOS or PMS, or a spreadsheet, that can help you here?). Try and plot your peaks and troughs on a chart (see Chapter 9 for some suggestions about presenting this). Do these occur at particular times of day or certain days of the week? Talk to your boss about whether you can increase customers in the low periods. If not, why not?

Special 'events' and offers

Special events can be good at attracting additional customers and persuading them to stay longer and spend more. Themed days or evenings can maximise revenues and satisfy customers, and in contract catering are good at preventing menu fatigue and encouraging customers to 'eat in' rather than bring their own. Special offers have a similar effect but can be run over a longer period – for instance a discount on a specific beer can be sponsored by a brewery, encourage more drinking and so generate more revenues and profits.

Daily specials on a menu can increase customers but more often will offer variety to existing customers (avoiding 'menu fatigue' which can cause numbers of customers to decrease). They also allow the business to use cheaper ingredients or use up excess stocks such as bin-ends. Happy hours are another way of encouraging more customers who hopefully will then continue to drink at full price.

Other special offers are geared at quiet times of the year. The 'lunch for a tenner' promotions, seen both nationally and locally, have been good at generating winter restaurant business. Customers often try a new venue and, if they like it, may well come back and spend ten times that on an evening meal in the future. This happens in all sectors in different ways – everybody has 'sales' of one type of another to encourage people to buy products or services.

Diversification of products

Here we mean offering different products to persuade them against going to a competitor. Offering alternatives to a captive audience can also help. Since many office workers often want to 'desk-dine' – eat a sandwich at their desk to save time – then many caterers have diversified their products by offering, say, a deli-bar, a sandwich shop, vending machines and perhaps a coffee shop in addition to the standard facilities. You do need to consider costs, though, if you are going to open satellite branches – sometimes they just aren't cost-effective.

Diversification of markets

Finding new markets can help improve revenues a lot, especially if your business is seasonal, as in a university town. Here local business must attract different types of customers, such as tourists, during holiday periods in order to maximise revenues in all aspects of hospitality – visitors will stay in hotels, eat in restaurants, drink in pubs, visit attractions, take tours and shop for souvenirs. Even schools may open for breakfast to increase sales and so cover more of the fixed costs (and there's an added bonus of ensuring the children are at school on time and aren't hungry).

Mini-case

An airport terminal had a satellite departure area with a snack bar. Unfortunately only a few flights a day (mostly in the evening) used this gate, but the authorities insisted on keeping the snack bar open all day 'just in case' passengers happened to wander down there while waiting for a flight at another gate.

The caterer argued that this was creating a loss as it was far too expensive for them to operate like this and it had a negative effect on passengers as they saw tired food and bored staff – but the authorities didn't see it that way.

The situation was only resolved when the airport increased its number of flights and had to use this satellite gate much more – with a consequent increase in sales for both caterer and airport authority.

Managing revenue

Discounts

Offering a discount can be a short-term way of encouraging business. Supermarkets are very good at persuading us to buy things and we can learn a lot from their techniques. The 'buy-one-get-one-free' offers aren't just designed to sell detergent or biscuits – you'll go in and buy other things as well. A good hospitality example is a hotel offering 'Sunday night at half price if you stay Friday and Saturday' – Sundays may be traditionally quiet and hotel guests usually spend money in the restaurant and bar especially if they have had a 'good deal' on their room.

Pizza restaurants can do it too on quieter days, or at slow times of the day (say mid-afternoon). If you take advantage of the offer then you will usually buy a drink and perhaps a dessert (with high GPs), which will be charged at full price and make profits for the business. Airlines offer discounts at quieter times of the week or year – it may seem a cheap flight but you could buy alcohol or perfume on board and if you like the airline return later for another, more expensive flight. The 'loss leader' approach works in hospitality too!

We'll look a bit more at how to ensure costs are still covered in the next two chapters.

Mini-case

A main-line rail station concourse was being redeveloped. The operators of the station thought that there were vast numbers of 'uncaptured' customers and that offering different products would expand the number of people buying food. In turn this might mean that they would spend money on other things too – all of which would mean more in the way of commission to themselves.

A supermarket was installed to the dismay of the existing outlets who saw the cheaper products available competing for their own business. These experienced operators immediately took action to change the type of product they sold so that they weren't competing – they identified new potential markets who would buy premium sandwiches, soup and snacks. They were happy, the supermarket was happy and the station operators were happier still (all the way to the bank).

Help from outside

'Mystery shoppers' are hired by the company to check on all aspects of service and control. A mystery shopper poses as a guest and observes incognito (without being rumbled) before reporting back on all aspects of the guest service and control to ensure everything is operating to standard.

There's a danger this can be used as a 'police officer' approach whereas it's better to consider this as another management tool that will highlight where things are going well, and where improvements are needed. They are trained in the business so will suggest informed improvements as well as pointing out issues.

Customer feedback

This can be really beneficial in telling you what customers think about your products and services and what's working and what's not. There are several ways of finding out – questionnaires, face-to-face discussion, focus groups and so on. See some of the books on the reading list for more details.

Activity

Next time you go out for a meal, why not be a 'mystery shopper'?

Do the staff try and optimise sales – sell you an extra bread roll or coffee after the meal, for instance? What about the marketing of the meal – does the menu entice you to eat? Does the ambience of the restaurant help you relax (or is it designed for high turnover so you're encouraged to eat up and get out as quickly as possible)? Would you return?

Is there anything you can learn from their sales and marketing techniques that will help you in your job? Are there any control issues you can spot – undercharging, for instance?

One more point. The 'quality experience' is intended to lead to a satisfied customer who will spend money, return at a future date, spend more money and then tell other people – it is normally far cheaper to keep an existing customer than to find a new one.

Exercise 3.2

Here's an exercise for you to do which will test a few of the skills covered in this (and the previous) Chapter. You can calculate variances and the percentage variance. You can then calculate the percentages to sales, and even the cost percentages – the same format applies. Lastly you can look at the other ratios and see if you can do those. Are there any more you could do?

BUT – what does this mean? Try and interpret the figures and identify where there are problems.

When you look at the answer you'll see some discussion about the variances and some ideas as to what may have happened.

Profit & Loss Report – Restaurant

28-day period	Budget		Actual		Variance	
Seats available per day	50		50			
Seats per 28-day period						
Covers sold	1,120		952			
Sales	(£)	(%)	(£)	(%)	(£)	(%)
Food	20,100		17,600			
Beverage	6,700		4,300			
Total						
Average spend/cover – food £p						
Average spend/cover – beverage £p						
Seat occupancy %						

Exercise 3.3: Staff dining facilities

Here's another exercise for you to try – please fill in all the boxes. You should first find the totals and then calculate some revenue ratios. (Assume the facilities are closed each month for 8 weekend days, plus the bank holiday in August)

		July	August	September
Days in month				
Sales		(£)	(£)	(£)
	Deli-bar	19,200	15,000	22,875
	Food hall	39,750	33,750	59,250
	Total			
Covers	Deli-bar	5,200	4,200	5,900
	Food hall	8,300	7,600	12,300
	Total			
		(£p)	(£p)	(£p)
Average Spends	Deli-bar			
	Food hall			
	Total			
Covers per day	Deli-bar			
	Food hall			
	Total			
		(£)	(£)	(£)
Sales per day	Deli-bar			
	Food hall			
	Total			

Summary

Within this third chapter we have focused on the revenue aspects of the hospitality business. Although some units or departments may not have sales there are still techniques here that may be helpful in the future. We have looked at both sales and control aspects and shown that the two cannot be treated independently – maximising revenue relies on good management practice from both perspectives. Use of ratios allows comparisons between budget and actual so managers can identify where action needs to be taken.

Revenue management as a topic is very complex and dynamic – there are new systems and approaches every few months. To find out more about it please look at industry articles and websites for up-to-date information.

In this chapter you have, therefore:

- Identified a range of revenue areas for the different sectors
- Examined a range of ratios that can be used to analyse revenues
- Identified the differences between revenue control and revenue management
- Discussed techniques for improving revenue gained from customers
- Discussed a variety of techniques to increase the number of customers.

Managing revenue

4 Managing costs

- Types of costs
- Ratios
- Control of costs
- Raw materials
- Labour
- Other costs

Introduction

In the previous chapter we discussed revenue and identified a range of areas where it can be improved by either sales or control techniques. However, in reality there may be only limited opportunities for you to improve revenues, or you may not have them at all. You then need to look at the other side of the P&L – costs. Controlling costs has always been more popular than controlling revenue with potentially large savings to be made by the manager, or so says the traditional view of the accountant.

In this chapter we'll look at the principles of controlling costs but within the constraints of maintaining the quality of customer service and product – which if not managed would result in an adverse effect on revenues. To do this we need to understand how costs behave, some being more controllable than others. You need to concentrate on managing what is manageable. As with revenue we'll also review the relevant ratios that will help indicate problems and then look at a range of techniques to minimise costs.

By the end of this chapter you will be able to:

- Identify the types of costs that occur in the various hospitality sectors
- Define cost behaviour and the difference between fixed and variable costs
- Calculate cost ratios
- Extract the fixed and variable elements from a series of total costs.

Types of costs

Many sectors rely on the effective control of costs in order to optimise the 'bottom line'. Managers can take simple actions which will have a significant effect on some of the costs, but other costs are relatively unmanageable. Hence, in order to target our attention and activities, we need to know which are *controllable*, and which are not. First, let's see the three main types of costs which are raw materials, labour and everything else (see Figure 4.1). We mentioned these in Chapter 2 when we looked at the P&L report. The 'everything else' can be split into departmental expenses, administrative expenses and property costs such as rent, rates and so on.

This type of classification doesn't really help us very much to manage costs because it doesn't tell you which you can control and which you can't (with the exception of the Fixed Charges below the GOP line, mentioned earlier). To really understand, we need to re-classify costs into how they behave.

Figure 4.1:
Types of costs

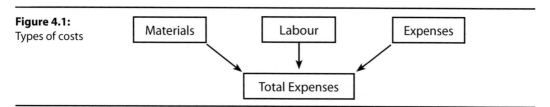

Costs can be *fixed*, *variable* or *semi-variable* (the terms 'mixed' or 'semi-fixed' are used in some textbooks).

Variable costs

Costs that are *variable* are totally dependent on the volume of sales. If you sell something then you incur a cost – so if you sell a bottle of cola you'll have the cost of that bottle. The raw materials that make food and beverage (the cost of sales, in other words) are the main type of variable cost but there are lots of other examples such as napkins, packaging for fast food, gift packs for guests, paper for printing tickets or guest bills. Some labour costs may be variable where you only employ staff if they have people to serve – banqueting is the most common example although takeaways try to operate on variable labour too.

These are relatively easy to manage as you shouldn't have a cost if there hasn't been a sale, but you do need to keep track of them to make sure things (such as bottles of cola) aren't going missing.

Fixed costs

Fixed costs, however, aren't affected by the volume of sales and so don't change much during the year. Typical examples are the fixed charges (rates, depreciation, and so on) already mentioned but there are also departmental and administrative costs, such as staff and management salaries, hire of equipment or flowers. It is difficult to manage these, as you must pay them no matter what the level of business in order to maintain quality.

Obviously if a staff member leaves then you can think about when or if you will recruit a replacement, but that's the only time you can easily reduce this cost (you wouldn't like it if your boss suddenly decided not to pay you if there wasn't enough business, would you?). Although making staff redundant may be an option, this can be expensive and time-consuming, as well as affecting the morale of all staff.

Semi-variable costs

Some costs are a mixture of fixed and variable and are called semi-variable – and so some parts are controllable and other parts aren't. For example, if you have a guest house then you need to have the lights on all the time in the entrance hall (fixed) but a bedroom light is only on when the room is occupied (variable). Another common example is staff pay – their basic wage is fixed but any overtime worked is variable.

Figure 4.2 extends the diagram in Figure 4.1.

Figure 4.2:
Types of costs

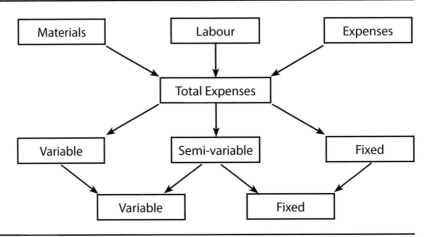

Other words you may hear quoted are 'direct' and 'indirect'. Direct costs are those able to be charged straight to a department. Indirect costs are generally those that belong to the property as a whole (including administration costs).

Different types of business

The disparate sectors all have these types but in varying proportions depending on how they operate – and so have different levels of controllability. In general, the higher priced the product is, the more likely the business is to have greater fixed than variable costs. This is because they tend to have a higher number of permanent well-trained (fixed) staff and also standard expenses (flowers and music all the time, for instance). Lower priced sectors, such as takeaways, are more likely to have variable paper goods or labour (part-time and with limited skills).

It may also be the particular location that affects the cost behaviour. If you have a remote site (an island, oil rig or middle of the desert, for instance) you often have to transport almost everything in, including the staff and all supplies. In these scenarios costs that might normally be variable can become semi-variable or fixed.

Ratios

As we did with revenue we can use ratios to identify where there are potential problems. These are mainly divided into two types – a cost per customer and a percentage. There are also productivity ratios related to how efficient your staff are in performing their jobs, although these aren't used in all sectors.

We'll look at overall cost ratios first and then within each section look at specific ones that apply to that type of cost. First we'll see the overall cost per customer ratios, which are exactly the same in concept as the revenue per customer ones we did in the last chapter – you take the amount and divide it by the number of people. Again the formula will be given first, followed by a short explanation.

Per customer costs

$$\text{Total cost per customer} \quad = \quad \frac{\text{Total cost } \pounds}{\text{Number of customers}} \quad \pounds p$$

This standard formula can be done per restaurant cover, fast food purchaser, theme park visitor, hotel guest, cruise ship passenger, staff eating in a catering facility – and so on. It's the total cost for any category on your P&L divided by the number of people served. The ratio is only appropriate (for control purposes) for those costs that are variable, so there's little point calculating the amount of depreciation cost per person, for instance.

As before these can be compared to your budget (and to last year) and a variance calculated. This will show you how much you have deviated in cost per customer from what you planned. If the cost is fully variable then there shouldn't be a variance – and you need to investigate why this has happened. Once you've identified a reason, you should (hopefully) be able to take action.

Some sectors use these cost calculations as the most important ratio and monitor not just individual amounts but the total costs per customer. For airline catering, for instance, even a five-pence variation can mean a high cost or saving when multiplied by thousands of meals a day.

Cost versus quality

Remember that spending too little can be as bad as spending too much – yes the costs are reduced but what has happened to the customer product or service? Has there been a decrease in quality? Has the portion of chips been reduced, a staff member underpaid or overworked (or both) or the sheets not changed? All these affect the 'guest experience' and ultimately revenue. So – lower costs need investigating as much as higher ones do.

The one problem with average cost amounts is that they need to be taken in the context of the sales figure – if the average revenue per customer rises then often so will the average cost. To monitor this you need to look at percentages too.

Cost percentages

$$\text{Cost of sales \% (CoS\%)} = \frac{\text{Total cost of sales £}}{\text{Sales £}} \, \%$$

$$\text{Gross profit \% (GP\%)} = \frac{\text{Gross profit £}}{\text{Sales £}} \, \%$$

As you see, you can take the total cost of sales and express it as a percentage of the sales. These two have been shown together because they are two aspects of the same approach. The cost percentage takes the cost as a percentage of sales whereas GP% looks at the gross profit as a percentage of sales – it really depends on the business that they focus on. A low cost % = a high GP%, and vice versa.

Most commercial businesses use a combination of average costs and percentages to highlight areas for action but, in order to take action you need to look at individual categories by themselves. Costs aren't always appropriate if sales have risen, whereas percentages only look at comparisons rather than at money amounts. Also, many managers are measured on their departmental cost percentages and a bad result can mean no bonus or a limited pay rise.

Control of costs

We will review these by category (raw materials, labour and other expenses) and consider how they can be controlled within the different sectors. We'll start with raw materials as these have the most stages to go through before the product is consumed. Labour is of course a part of this too but has fewer stages where controls are needed. The other costs will be reviewed last as, although they aren't usually as significant as the others, they still need to be effectively managed. You'll see some more relevant ratios and we will then discuss potential problems and suggest some solutions (there's more in other chapters).

Small businesses often have very few types of costs (a guesthouse, for instance only offers a room and breakfast, and perhaps dinner) and these should be easy to control, especially if the owner is also the manager. Even here, however, there will be opportunities to trim costs, perhaps by the use of flexible labour and the purchase of food only when it is needed.

Raw materials

As mentioned in Chapter 2, raw materials are 'cost of sales'. We will mainly concentrate on food and beverages but others (such as telephone) will be discussed briefly as well.

Ratios for raw materials

As we've seen, these costs are usually variable and so are directly proportional to the number of meals (or drinks) that are provided for customers, whether for money or not. The main two ratios that are used are cost of food or beverage per customer and the food or beverage cost percentage.

$$\text{Food cost per customer (or any other)} = \frac{\text{Total food cost £}}{\text{Number of customers}} \quad \text{£p}$$

$$\text{Cost per meal*} = \frac{\text{Total cost for meal £}}{\text{Number of meals}} \quad \text{£p}$$

*(if more than one meal per person, e.g. on a long-haul flight or package break, or in a residential home)

Cost per person (or meal) is used extensively in cost-sector catering where there is a specific amount allowed per meal or per day – and this may be subsidised.

It's less popular in commercial environments, where they are more likely to use percentages. The chef on a cruise ship normally has a budget of a food cost per passenger per day to feed the vast number and variety of meals that are served during the day – all included in the price of the cruise. This can be up to seven meals a day (does anybody eat that much?).

$$\text{Food cost percentage (also beverage, phone, laundry, etc)} = \frac{\text{Food cost of sales £}}{\text{Food sales £}} \quad \%$$

$$\text{Beverage gross profit (also food and others, as above)} = \frac{\text{Beverage gross profit £}}{\text{Beverage sales £}} \quad \%$$

These are the most important percentages of all for catering areas and show the cost of the raw materials consumed (or the GP – which depends on the focus of the business) in relation to the sales. Different sectors will, of course, work towards different percentages. Some have to achieve the same cost percentage on all items but it is more common to have different percentages for different items. A university food facility (which is subsidised) may have a 60% food cost whereas a pasta restaurant can work to 30%.

Even within a single unit, different meals and dishes can have lower food cost (usually expressed as 'higher GP') – so a hotel breakfast has a much higher GP than lunch, and an orange juice in a cafe a lower GP than a cup of tea. For an explanation of why this happens then please see Chapter 5, on pricing.

Overall cost averages for your entire stock really aren't good enough as they can hide where a problem occurs. For instance, would you notice a 1% fall in GP if you have a very big turnover – but convert this into money and you will see the value of what you have lost? Here's an example:

	(£)
Sales for a month	500,000
Cost of sales at 34%	170,000
Cost of sales at 35%	175,000
Difference (Loss!)	5,000

Five thousand pounds would pay your wages for several months.

As an example we can add to the restaurant exercise from the previous chapter. Note that the cost of sales % (and GP%) on food is calculated as a proportion of food sales (and beverage costs to beverage sales), not total sales.

	Budget		Actual		Variance	%
Covers sold	1,120		952		(168)	(15.0)
Revenue	(£)	(%)	(£)	(%)	(£)	(%)
Food	20,100	75.0	17,600	80.4	(2,500)	(12.4)
Beverage	6,700	25.0	4,300	19.6	(2,400)	(35.8)
Total	26,800	100.0	21,900	100.0	(4,900)	(18.3)
Cost of sales						
Food	(10,000)	(49.8)	(7,900)	(44.9)	2,100	21.0
Beverage	(2,670)	(39.9)	(1,620)	(37.7)	1,050	39.3
Total	(12,670)	(47.3)	(9,520)	(43.5)	3,150	24.9
Gross profit						
Food	10,100	50.2	9,700	55.1	(400)	(4.0)
Beverage	4,030	60.1	2,680	62.3	(1,350)	(33.5)
Total	14,130	52.7	12,380	56.5	(1,750)	(12.4)
Total cost of sales/cover	11.31		10.00		(1.31)	(11.6)
Total gross profit/cover	12.62		13.00		0.39	3.1

Attitudes to control

Attitudes to food by staff can be tricky – do they see it as fuel, as an item they prepare or sell, or as a reward? They may not think of it as having value, and so consider it as consumable.

> **Mini-case**
>
> A well-patronised restaurant used a lot of student labour who were not well paid. They relied on their tips to help them fund their studies, and on the meal that they ate while working. A new manager wasn't happy, though, when he realised that the staff were eating the very expensive cakes intended for customers and spoiling the display at the same time. Supplies for guests were running out and these weren't being costed for in the staff meal allowance – result: unhappy guests and a high food cost. He explained to the staff (carefully!) that they weren't entitled to cake and that if head office found out they would consider this as stealing. The staff hadn't thought of it this way and certainly hadn't considered the financial implications. They often didn't even eat all the cakes, they just wanted a taste.
>
> A compromise was reached. The staff ate ice-cream as part of the staff meal, and each day they all shared a guest dessert so that they could see what it was like and recommend it to customers.

Attitudes to drink vary by sector. In pubs and clubs there's a tradition of staff drinking with customers although many businesses now limit the amount of alcohol consumed as too much of it can affect your ability to do the job. It also costs the business less if staff have soft drinks or water – they're not 'drinking away the profits' any more.

The main problem is that you just can't check everything, as we discussed in the previous chapter. With costs, as with revenue, you have to be able to trust your staff. MBWA ('management by walking about') helps with costs too, but so does the 'lead from the top' approach. If managers behave honestly and efficiently then most employees will do so too. That said, some types of operation are more susceptible to theft than others – with pubs often being notorious for losses of stock. Some of this is due to drinking on duty, others to the desirability and portability of the product (particularly spirits). It doesn't help when shortfalls on gross profits are called 'shrinkage', which disguises the fact that wastage and fraud may be occurring and that these are controllable.

Ways of improving GPs

We discuss production and portion control further in Chapter 8, on standard costing, and stock usage in Chapter 7 on cash and stocks.

Knowing what's profitable

Electronic Point of Sale (EPOS) systems help you analyse what is selling well and, if programmed with costs for each item, will show you the most and least profitable items and the overall GPs achieved.

You then use your selling skills to persuade people to buy things that have a lower cost, such as own label products or 'specials'. It's most common in food and beverage (it's called menu engineering) but is also applicable to other sectors. Remember that you can often achieve a higher GP at different times of day due to price sensitivity – you may be able to charge more for the same item in the evening, for instance, than you can at lunchtime.

Mystery shoppers (mentioned in the last chapter) are often used in bars to monitor not only the sales but also the costs – they'll watch bar staff to see how honest and efficient they are. If it's your own pub then you could ask a friend (who's not known to your staff) to come and be a customer for you and see what's happening.

Mini-case

Buffet crews on one railway line relate how, if the stores staff at their base station forget to load a trolley on their train early in the morning, first-class passengers don't receive their advertised free at-seat trolley service of beverages and biscuits. They then have to be served with standard products, reducing availability for other passengers – which in turn leads to disgruntled passengers and control problems for the crew.

Relationship between costs

One more thing to think about. Sometimes a high food (or beverage) cost can be offset by lower labour costs – so you need to think overall rather than in isolation. Buffet meals are a good example – they are very high in food cost due to the wastage element, but the labour cost is minimal. Buying-in prepared products is expensive on food cost but saves on kitchen labour, and so on. Mini bars are very expensive staff-wise to replenish on a daily basis so most hotels will only do this after the guest departs. Most guests are honest, but some aren't, and you do need to factor into the cost the loss you will make from some guests. It may be worthwhile trying to identify if particular types of guests are more likely to cheat than others – and targeting their rooms for daily inspections.

Also, hospitals may have volunteers to help on wards with consequent savings on labour. Unfortunately these 'staff' may not have any knowledge of control and so, for instance, give a larger drink of orange juice than is budgeted for.

Other types of 'raw materials'

Telephone units

In a hotel or similar establishments where telephones are installed in rooms, the guests are charged a premium rate for the calls they make. This can be several times the cost of using a mobile phone but establishments argue that the charge is subsidising the cost of providing the switchboard service, and so on.

The cost of the units counts as 'cost of sales' and is expressed as a percentage as are other costs. It's a fully variable cost too – the unit charge is only imposed when a call is made. Most establishments use computerised systems that automatically charge the call to the guest room, so losses are minimal, but this service rarely makes a profit due to low levels of usage. The majority of business – and leisure – guests use their own mobile phones for calls, so only where telecommunications reception is poor is a hotel system likely to have much usage .

Guest laundry and dry-cleaning

This is normally 'contracted out' whereby the items are sent to an external company for cleaning. The company will make a charge to the hotel (or apartment) which then forms the 'cost price'. This is grossed up (see Chapter 5 on pricing on how to do this) to give a selling price which is charged to the guest bill. Again, the only potential savings are in finding a cheaper supplier but here quality of service is more important than cost – to both hotel and guest.

In-room entertainment

The last major area where you can find cost of sales is in-room entertainment which includes both pay-per-view movies and Internet access (usually wireless) for which many hotels make a charge. Again the charge to the guest includes the equipment rental and may well subsidise the provision of cable and satellite channels, for instance. The system will be linked to the PMS at front desk, providing automatic charging for whichever options the guest chooses .

Labour

Payroll can be the biggest expense of all – in some sectors such as hospital cleaning it can represent 90% of the total costs. Even in commercial catering it can represent 30% of sales. There are some controls that you can put in place but often there is a minimum staffing requirement due to health and safety legislation, hygiene rules or standards of service.

Much payroll is fixed in nature, with staff being employed on permanent contracts, particularly in the UK. Other countries often have more 'flexible' approaches to contracts, and there's a trend towards these in some sectors here too. Part of the problem though is the different attitudes of staff and management – what managers see as flexible working a staff member may see as exploitation.

Ratios

Here are the main ratios that are used to measure overall payroll cost:

$$\text{Payroll \%} = \frac{\text{Payroll cost £}}{\text{Sales £}} \quad \%$$

$$\text{Payroll cost per customer} = \frac{\text{Payroll cost £}}{\text{Customers}} \quad \text{£p}$$

These are similar to the ratios we've already looked at. The last, non-monetary, type of ratio is productivity. We've seen that you can calculate a payroll cost or percentage, but you can also look at staffing in terms of time.

Here are a couple of examples:

$$\text{Time taken to serve a customer} = \frac{\text{Number of customers}}{\text{Time}} \quad \text{(mins \& secs)}$$

$$\text{Meals per labour hour} = \frac{\text{Number of meals}}{\text{Number of hours}}$$
(used a lot in cost sector catering)

Here you are seeing the average time taken to do a job. You might also want to see how many tasks a person does in a day:

$$\text{Rooms cleaned per staff member} = \frac{\text{Number of rooms}}{\text{Number of staff}}$$

$$\text{Meals prepared per staff member} = \frac{\text{Number of meals}}{\text{Number of staff}}$$

For example – if you have 5 staff preparing 2000 sandwiches a day then the ratio would be:

$$\text{Sandwiches prepared per staff member} = \frac{\text{Number of meals}}{\text{Number of staff}} = \frac{2000}{5} = 400 \text{ each}$$

Fixed payroll

This generally means the salaries and wages of all permanent staff which in many businesses is the majority of employees, whether full or part time. They are often perceived as more stable and more reliable than 'casual' staff which is good for maintaining service standards but can be difficult cost wise. Also, the higher the grade of establishment the more likely there is to be more permanent, fixed staffing – and so payroll cost.

Pay rates in different areas of the country vary (for the same job) and accordingly will also affect the payroll costs, although all staff must earn at least the minimum wage level . In sectors such as cruise-lines, staff tend to be employed from nations where pay rates are lower than some western countries, which can also reduce costs.

Given the high proportion of fixed payroll in many sectors, managing the cost can be tricky. There are things you can do, however, without the need for redundancies:

☐ Use of forecasting techniques to predict the level of business can help you to schedule staff more efficiently. If you know, for instance, that you are likely to have a quiet period ahead then you can persuade staff to take holidays or bank holidays that they are owed.

☐ Some types of business have traditional peaks and troughs at different times of year. For instance, pubs and restaurants tend to be very busy in the weeks leading up to Christmas so staff have little time off. In the New Year, however, they can be much quieter and so the staff can take the time that they are owed.

☐ If you are able to negotiate with your staff you can offer to give them time off in lieu rather than pay overtime, so that they can take several days off together.

☐ If a member of staff leaves, do you have to replace them immediately? If business looks quieter then you may be able to manage without that post for a couple of months or so. For management positions it may take you that long to recruit anyway.

☐ You can employ new members of staff on lower pay rates – but you need to be very careful here. Sometimes this can be legitimate if the leaver was entitled to long-service bonuses or enhancement but if the business is unionised then there may well be an agreed rate for each job. There are now established legal precedents that mean that staff should maintain terms and conditions when new caterers take over a contract.

☐ One other approach is to keep a minimum permanent staff and then ask them to work overtime when it's busy. You need to recognise though that staff are often more efficient if they work shorter hours – working overtime (paid or unpaid) just makes them tired and less efficient. This applies to you too!

Managing costs

Part time and flexible payroll

There are two approaches to flexible working – flexible jobs and flexible hours.

Flexible jobs have always been used in smaller units but in recent years has become more prevalent in larger units. Everybody may now be multi-skilled so that they can help out where needed.

Mini-case

A large hotel situated next to a Premier League football club tends to get very busy on match days. When this happens all the available staff and managers are expected to help the bar staff clear glasses and change ashtrays. Once the match has started the room attendants join the porters in cleaning the floor, toilets and tables so that the area will look 'normal' again as quickly as possible. This isn't seen as just work – it's everybody pulling together for the benefit of all. Staff enjoy doing different jobs occasionally.

You can offer *flexible hours* on a permanent or non-permanent (short-term contract) basis. This can be very efficient in keeping costs under control when you have variable levels of business (but note that the entitlement for benefits is normally the same as for permanent and full-time staff). You have to balance this flexibility with staff morale – if staff are happy with this type of contract then it may be the best solution but there is a danger that they may become demoralised and leave for more stable employment.

Students, for instance, frequently work during their holiday periods or at weekends on short-term contracts to fill in while permanent staff are on holiday or days off. Working parents often need hours to fit in child-care and so you can juggle different types of workforce at different times.

Lower grade establishments tend to operate with more flexible payroll – staff on variable contracts who move jobs frequently. Although this means that you can control the costs more easily (e.g. not hiring when you don't need them) there's a trade-off in lack of reliability and levels of skills. Skilled staff are more likely to want (and be able to secure) permanent employment with good benefits and career prospects. Fast food takeaways often advertise for staff for a limited number of hours per day – say to cover lunch-time peaks. They can't afford to employ staff who aren't busy.

Activity

Do you know of any businesses that operate with a flexible workforce? Look out on the high street for advertisements for staff – they will often say 'hours to suit' from 2 to 30 hours per week – or similar. They look like they're being flexible for the employee, but really it's to help manage their payroll cost.

Contracting out or outsourcing labour or other services

It can be cheaper to 'contract out' (outsource) some services as well as payroll, and certainly easier. Laundering of bedlinen and table linen, for instance, often used to be done 'in-house' which can still be cost-effective if you have the facilities. Most of this is contracted out now to specialists because of the problems in hiring trained staff, the space that is required and the environmental issues associated with chemicals and water. For very small businesses (like a bed and breakfast) it still may be quicker to do it yourself in a domestic washer, but for larger units the volumes of linen required are enormous (think about a 500-person banquet and the napkins and cloths required, and then needing the same again the next day).

Cleaning of public areas is also often contracted out to specialist cleaners who visit at quiet times (often the middle of the night). There have been some experiments with contracting out cleaning on a large scale and these have been successful in some areas (such as hospitals and schools) but less so in hotels. This may be because of the higher quality of furnishings, security issues in accessing guest property or because of the nature of the business (open 24 hours, for instance).

Other services may be outsourced when specialist help is needed. An organisation may decide that it is easier to have an external company preparing their payroll, for instance, where specialist tax and legal issues are prevalent. Outsourcing IT is common, whether for full software provision or just data storage, and accounting and revenue management functions are also found, saving staff and money.

Some larger companies may 'in-source' which means having a separate division that provides the required service. This division may be run semi-independently, with expert staff, and will charge the individual unit for the services required. The company sees the benefit of economies of scale whilst still retaining in-house control.

Labour outsourcing can be approached through de-skilling, contract labour or casuals.

De-skilling

A lot of kitchens have 'contracted out' the preparation of food items and now buy in items such as meat pre-prepared. Few kitchens have a full pastry section now – they buy their cakes from specialist bakers. The cost of materials is higher but there is a saving on payroll costs and on the space required. Although there are benefits for the business there's a danger the chefs themselves may feel under-used and under-valued if their skills are no longer necessary.

Managing costs

Contract staff

You can hire staff in from an agency to do a variety of jobs, or hire a firm for a particular area. Agency staff can work in housekeeping, administration, on food counters and as drivers. You might hire a specialist company to clean your carpets, maintain your electrical or catering equipment or to run your recruitment campaign. The supplier contracts to provide the service and you have to pay the bill. Although expensive it can be cost-effective especially if you need technical expertise.

Casual staff

These are the traditional way of managing payroll in a variable-volume situation. The most common area is in banqueting where staff are hired purely for a specific function but may also be used to fill in gaps when regular staff are on holiday or sick. Many may be hired via an agency but this can be expensive so a unit may have its own list of casual staff it can call if needed.

Event catering peaks in the summer for outdoor events and for these few weeks you may have a team of casuals who work on a series of functions. Revenue and Customs insist that casuals are paid via the payroll and have tax deducted so that they are legal employees. The more formal nature of their employment has meant a more stable workforce with casuals now being considered as part of the staff, albeit often with irregular hours. Costs have increased (for pay, uniforms, meals, training, etc.) but so has the quality of service.

Activity   Are any of your staff or services contracted out or outsourced in any way? Can you identify why this is?

Employee benefits

Payroll cost isn't just the cost of the wages – there are all the 'benefits' (or 'on-cost') that have to be added to the overall cost of employing someone. The cost of this averages about an extra 20% – less for a part-timer and more for a manager. Another payroll ratio that may be relevant is the percentage of benefits to basic pay.

A manager employed overseas on an 'ex-pat' package can have a benefits package larger than their salary. This can include annual travel for the whole family back to their home country, housing, health care, school fees, company cars and so on – it gets *very* expensive to employ ex-pats, so you have to be sure that they are worth it.

Some other examples of benefits are:

Holiday pay	Travel home late at night
Sick pay	Subsidised loans for travel or mortgages
Maternity pay	Staff accommodation
Paternity pay	Staff meals (though not all staff have these now)
Parental leave	Company cars
Subsidised child care	Mobile phones
Bonuses	Private health care
Pension contributions	Uniforms
National Insurance (another employment tax)	Subsidised or free laundry or dry cleaning
Life assurance	

Activity　　What sort of benefits do you have? Is it just meals on duty, a uniform, holiday and sick pay or are there more? Do you have to pay a contribution towards any of these – if so, do you know why? (Hint – it's a tax issue.)

Training

The cost of training can be regarded in different ways. To some it's a benefit, and so it classed as part of payroll. To other businesses it's an overall business cost as training affects all areas. It can be thought of as very controllable, and in difficult trading periods is often one of the first costs to be cut – *but* there is a load of (often anecdotal) evidence to suggest that better trained employees bring in better sales and costs. On one hand employers complain that 'they can't get the trained staff' and yet on the other don't put the investment into staff training. You'll see frequent letters and articles about this topic if you read the trade press regularly.

There's a tendency to concentrate on health and safety and fire training (the ones required by law) and leave other training to just 'happen'. Staff then vote with their feet – if they aren't invested in (that is, trained and developed) then they won't stay. This is considered more in the final chapter. Training is crucial to ensure good cost control. This can be in terms of attitude (zero tolerance of theft, for instance) or in skills such as cleaning silver and glassware (which can be very expensive and easily breakable), portion control or use of paper goods.

Other costs

You have seen the overall cost per customer and cost percentages that were calculated earlier. You can use these formulas to calculate individual costs too. Costs for departments are calculated as a percentage of the departmental sales, but for administration as a percentage of the total unit sales.

Again costs are split into fixed and variable and we will consider some of the types of costs that occur in each of these classifications. Remember though that cost behaviour differs by sector (and sometimes by season) and so what may be classified as variable in one situation may be fixed in another. As we've seen, in general the higher the 'grade' of business the more fixed costs they have in order to maintain their established standards.

Variable costs

You need to establish exactly which costs are variable in your business and then decide how much you need to spend on each item – this is part of setting standards. This is likely to be dependent on actual items so you need to work out what you need as well as how much it will cost. So – how many paper napkins do you need on average per customer? Is it one each, or do they take more? What quality – one-ply is far cheaper, but two-ply feels more luxurious – three-ply even more so? Do you give straws with your soft drinks? How many tablets of soap does each guest need? How many times do you change the sheets (every day in a five-star hotel but only on departure in a guest house)? Do you need branded products – they may be expensive but they are also a marketing technique.

You can calculate these costs individually by customer or by percentage as well. For example:

$$\text{Paper cost \%} = \frac{\text{Paper Cost £}}{\text{Sales £}} \, \%$$

$$\text{Paper cost per customer} = \frac{\text{Paper Cost £}}{\text{Customers}} \, £p$$

Once your standards are established you need to communicate this to your staff so they know too – and then monitor that this is happening. If different rules apply to different types of customers then this needs to be clear too (business guests get shampoo and conditioner in their rooms but tour groups only get shampoo; the directors dining room has linen tablecloths *and* napkins *and* silver cutlery but everybody else has bare tables, paper napkins and stainless steel cutlery).

Rent

One more cost that may sometimes be variable is rent. If you pay a fixed rental (probably on a square metre basis) then this counts as a fixed cost. If, however, your rent is based on a percentage of sales then it is fully variable. Management contracts often operate in this way and so do retail or catering units in shopping centres and airports. The rent can be as high as 25% of sales in some cases.

Fixed costs

Many departmental costs are fixed as we saw earlier. You need to keep the lighting and heating on in your building whenever you are open, and floors in a cafeteria or hostel need cleaning every day. Even if a hospital ward is 'closed' it still needs some attention to keep it clean. Motorway service areas are another example, they don't just operate the catering outlets but have to offer all the other facilities on the site, on a 24-hour basis – the shops, toilets, parking, fuel and amusements. The costs of running these are nearly all fixed – it doesn't matter whether it's the middle of the night or the middle of the day they still need to be open for business. Event caterers need to transport all equipment and materials to the location, which incurs fixed costs such as refrigeration, electricity and running costs for the van. These may vary with the size and distance to the event but are still essentially fixed in nature.

Managing costs

You can try to manage fixed costs to some extent – often by planning ahead. By finding the cheapest place to purchase your products you may be able to cut costs. For instance, using an alternative supplier for utilities (electricity, gas, water or telephone) may help you to trim the cost. You can also consider using a lower specification (such as lower-strength light bulbs) or look long-term and try to save costs by installing new equipment or changing behaviour. Again with utilities, modern boiler systems can cut energy usage dramatically, and training staff to only switch on gas ovens when needed saves costs as well as helping the environment.

Recycling, while also environmentally friendly is also financially beneficial. In the past there has been extensive wastage of all types of resource within the unit. By re-using and recycling you can save costs as well. You can re-use paper for message pads, recycle bottles and cans and cut down on printing by keeping most records electronically rather than hard-copy. You can cut old large linen tablecloths into smaller ones, and then into napkins and eventually they can get used up for kitchen cloths.

Another approach that companies may consider to help save costs is outsourcing (contracting out) which we looked at earlier.

Seasonality

Some businesses are highly seasonal which affects their cost structures. Traditionally, many seaside hotels used to close in winter due to low occupancies but now tend to remain open and to look for new markets that will generate some revenue to cover their fixed operating costs. Apartment complexes and large hotels in resort areas can offer economies of scale in that a relatively small management team can operate a large number of room blocks and other facilities. Operative staff may be hired on a flexible, perhaps seasonal, basis so the opportunity is available to open and close different areas according to demand.

Exercise 4.1

Using the restaurant exercise again, let's add some more costs. Please calculate the profit and percentages as well.

	Budget		Actual		Variance	Variance %
Seats available	50		50			
Seats per period	1,400		1,400		0	0.0
Covers sold	1,120		952		(168)	(15.0)
	(£)	(%)	(£)	(%)	(£)	(%)
Sales						
Food	20,100	75.0	17,600	80.4	(2,500)	(12.4)
Beverage	6,700	25.0	4,300	19.6	(2,400)	(35.8)
Total	26,800	100.0	21,900	100.0	(4,900)	(18.3)
Cost of sales						
Food	(10,000)	(49.8)	(7,900)	(44.9)	2,100	21.0
Beverage	(2,670)	(39.9)	(1,620)	(37.7)	1,050	39.3
Total	(12,670)	(47.3)	(9,520)	(43.5)	3,150	24.9
Gross profit						
Food	10,100	50.2	9,700	55.1	(400)	(4.0)
Beverage	4,030	60.1	2,680	62.3	(1,350)	(33.5)
Total	14,130	52.7	12,380	56.5	(1,750)	(12.4)
Payroll cost	(9,520)		(8,400)		1,120	
Departmental expenses	(2,100)		(1,600)		500	
Food & beverage profit						

	(£)		(£)		(£)	(%)
Payroll cost per cover						
Expenses cost per cover						
Profit per cover						

Fixed charges

These really can be difficult to manage and you do need to think a long way ahead if you are to minimise these costs. Here are some ideas:

☐ Interest payments – it may be possible to negotiate a lower rate

☐ Rent can be re-negotiated – and do you really need an expensive high-street location anyway? Must you provide staff accommodation in rented houses, or can you find an alternative?

☐ Depreciation is based on buying fixed assets. In future, could equipment be leased or hired? This will help your cash situation as well as reducing the depreciation (though you'd still have rental costs).

☐ It may be possible to get business rates reduced, with negotiation, if you can prove that they are higher than those of equivalent businesses in the area.

Activity   Find three expense items in your area that you think could be better managed in terms of cost. Suggest these to your manager. There may be other reasons that you aren't aware of for high costs, but at least this will develop your awareness.

Exercise 4.2: Town centre department store

Here's another exercise. Do the figures, then look at what they mean. Focus on the payroll and the cost of sales, and try and see what's happening.

	March (£)	March (%)	April (£)	April (%)	May (£)	May (%)
Sales						
Cafe	9,000		10,500		12,000	
Restaurant	12,000		15,000		21,000	
Total						
Cost of sales						
Cafe	(4,500)		(5,670)		(6,840)	
Restaurant	(4,800)		(6,300)		(9,030)	
Total						
Gross profit						
Cafe	4,500		4,830		5,160	
Restaurant	7,200		8,700		11,970	
Total						
Wages						
Overtime	(5,250)		(5,860)		(4,485)	
Net profit	(450)		(530)		(2,115)	
Covers						
Cafe	3,750		4,667		5,714	
Restaurant	1,667		2,128		3,043	
Total						

	(£)	(£)	(£)
Average spends			
Cafe			
Restaurant			
Total			
Gross profit/cover			
Cafe			
Restaurant			
Total			
Wages/cover			
Overtime/cover			
Net profit/cover			

Summary

In this chapter we've looked at the principles of managing costs. We have:

- Reviewed the differences between fixed and variable costs and identified some within your own area
- Discussed how different costs are classified
- Calculated ratios that assist in controlling costs
- Discussed the role of the manager in controlling costs
- Identified some specific ways in which the manager can control raw materials, labour and other costs.

5 Pricing to achieve profit

- Different types of pricing
- Marketer's methd of pricing
- Fitting the methods together
- Breaking even

Introduction

One of the most important techniques for managers to understand is how to price a product to attract customers – and also to achieve a profit (or at least cover all the costs). If you can be aware of all the different factors that influence a price (and not just what the customer is prepared to pay) then you will be able to generate both revenue and profit from your products and services.

Another helpful technique is to know how many you need to sell of a product or service at a given price to cover all the costs – this is called the 'break-even point'.

By the end of this chapter you will be able to:

- Describe the factors that influence pricing decisions
- Identify the most appropriate pricing method for a product or service
- Calculate a price to achieve a profit
- Calculate how many products or services you need to sell to reach the break-even point.

Different types of pricing

There are two different approaches used in pricing – which can be generally described as the 'accountant's method' and the 'marketer's method'. Traditionally the two are seen as totally different, but we will try and make them fit together in order to satisfy the needs of both. We'll also look briefly at putting package prices together. We will look at the 'accountant's method' first, which uses costs as the basis for calculating a selling price. This is known as 'cost-plus'.

One item to note: the selling price is the price the business receives and does not include any VAT (Value Added Tax), which needs to be added on afterwards to give a 'price charged to the customer' which you would display on a menu or tariff board.

Cost-plus pricing

For this method the most important factor is the costs identified with producing (or buying-in) the product and then a margin, or 'mark-up' is added on to cover all other costs and the profit to arrive at the selling price. There are three main types of cost-plus pricing – gross profit, contribution margin and bottom-up methods.

Gross profit method

This is the most common method used in pricing food and beverage products, and is very simplistic in its approach. It uses only the cost of the raw materials, with the margin that is added covering all other costs (variable and fixed) and the profit required. Look at Figure 5.1.

Figure 5.1: Gross profit pricing

In this type of pricing the margin is the same as the GP achieved – hence the name – and this margin is normally quoted as a percentage of the selling price, e.g. a pint of beer:

	(£)	(%)
Cost of beer	0.85	35.0
Margin (GP)	1.58	65.0
Selling price	2.43	100.0

(If you then added VAT at 20% you'd have a price to the customer of £2.92 – more than three times the actual cost of the beer. For wines in restaurants it's quite common to pay four or five times the amount you would pay in a supermarket for the same bottle of wine.)

Tip

To add VAT at 20% on to a selling price to reach the 'menu price' or 'price charged to the customer', take the selling price and multiply it by 1.2 – that gives you the final number you need. The amount of VAT is the difference between the first and the second figures.

There are no 'standard' cost percentages for products – it will vary according to the type of operation, location and so on. You'll see this more when we look at market-based pricing.

Contribution margin method

GP pricing only uses the raw materials – and ignores all other variable costs such as wages, paper goods, give-aways, linen, transport and so on (these are covered by the margin, mentioned above). A better approach would be to take all of the variable costs into the calculation – this is called contribution pricing. Here the 'cost base' is all the variable costs, which we discussed earlier. Using this method the margin then covers the fixed costs and the profit required (see Figure 5.2).

Figure 5.2: Contribution pricing

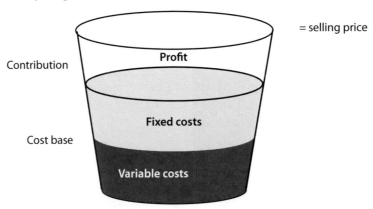

You can use this method where you have a lot of variable costs – such as a fast-food operation, a day trip or a package holiday. For example, for a burger bar:

	(£)	(%)
Variable costs – burger, bun, sauce, garnish, chips, drink, packaging, labour and so on	2.04	60.0
Contribution	1.36	40.0
Selling price	3.40	100.0
Plus VAT at 20% = Menu price	4.08	

Where the business has a wide range of products this method is still feasible. A theme park, for example, may have lots of rides, retail shops, food outlets and vending machines but should still be able to identify all the different variable costs associated with each type. The only minor drawback of both these methods is that they assume that the cost of the individual items will be the same – which is also unrealistic. Given that items such as food change their cost daily it is inevitable that the profit will change daily too – and so the GP or contribution achieved is only an average over a period and can't be considered totally accurate.

Again, do you use this method? Would it be more appropriate than GP pricing? Can you think of any other product or service that could use it?

Exercise 5.1: Pricing a take-away coffee

Work through the exercse,then check your answer with the one at the end of the book.

Number sold	5,000
Food cost per cup	£0.25
Labour cost per cup	£0.20
Paper and other supplies per cup	£0.07
Fixed costs (total)	£5,000
Profit required per cup	£0.25

What price should be charged, including VAT?

You can do this in two ways. The easiest is to work out the fixed cost per cup, the profit per cup, then add all the costs and profit together to reach a selling price. Then you would add the VAT. Alternatively you could multiply out the number of cups times the food cost, paper cost and so on to get the total costs, and then divide that by the number of cups to reach a per item price.

Here's a grid for the first method (fill in the boxes, please):

Coffees		5,000
	Total	Per cup
	(£)	(£)
Fixed costs	£5,000	
Profit required		£0.25
Variable costs		
Food		
Labour		
Paper		
Add all these together to get a selling price		
Add the VAT (multiply by 1.2)		

Grossing up

Sometimes you just have the cost amount and you need to achieve a certain contribution percentage (or GP percentage). For this you need to gross up the cost amount to reach the selling price.

What if you had a £23.50 variable cost and wanted to achieve an 80% contribution on sales?

- the variable percentage is 20% (selling price = 100% less contribution 80%)

If you *divide* the cost by the percentage that it represents you will find out the gross amount

---

Tip

To divide by a percentage, using a calculator (and the figures in the example below) press '23.50' (the variable cost on this examples), then the divide button, then '20' and finally the '%' button. This gives you a figure of 117.50.

So the selling price (before VAT) will be:

$$\frac{\text{Variable cost £}}{\text{Variable cost \%}} = \frac{£23.50}{20\%} = £117.50 \text{ selling price}$$

Assume you had a £7.75 laundry cost and wanted to achieve a 35% cost of sales. What is the selling price?

- this £7.75 cost represents 35% of the selling price (which = 100%).

So:

$$\frac{\text{Cost price £}}{\text{Cost price \%}} = \frac{£7.75}{35\%} = £22.14 \text{ selling price} \quad \text{inc. VAT} = £26.57 \text{ (or £26.60?)}*$$

*on the guest laundry list

(You can check it back – deduct the VAT at 20% to get to the selling price. Take the £22.14 and multiply it by 35% to see the laundry cost in £).

Tip

To deduct VAT from a customer price:

Take the customer price and *divide* it by 1.2 to get back to the selling price – the reverse of adding the VAT as you did before.

Exercise 5.2

A guest house has variable costs of £32.45 and wants to achieve a contribution of 45%. What's the selling price – and the price charged to the customer?

Bottom-up method

The last cost-plus method is known as 'bottom-up' pricing (also known as the Hubbart formula). It is mainly used for new projects, particularly hotels, where you need to know in advance whether you will achieve the required return (profit) on your investment.

The best description is that it is an 'upside-down' P&L report, and it is almost always used by consultants when looking at 'new builds'. They use standard average costs – benchmarks – from published industry reports so that they can compare one project to another. Within an existing business you might want to use this for a refurbishment project, for instance, or an extension, in which case your accounts office should have figures available.

To calculate it (this example is for a new hotel) you need to start with the profit you want, add back the tax and then the costs until you reach the revenue needed (subtracting any secondary departments on the way). Once you have the revenue you can divide this by the expected rooms sold to reach an average room rate.

Here's a grid layout:

Return on investment required

+ Tax payable

= **Profit before tax** _____

+ Fixed costs

+ Administration & other cost

= **Departmental operating profit** _____

– Food & beverage dept profit

– Sundry dept profit _____

= **Rooms department profit**

+ Rooms expenses _____

= **Rooms revenue**

Rooms available × occupancy % = rooms sold

$$\text{Rooms revenue} \quad = \quad \frac{\text{average room rate required}}{\text{Rooms sold}}$$

The only tricky bit is adding back the tax at the beginning. To do this requires the grossing up technique that we did earlier:

Profit after tax required by the investors (PaT), £2,000,000 and tax rate 28%.

Using grossing up you need to find the profit before tax (PbT). This will be 100% before the 28% is deducted – and hence the PaT amount will be 72%.

$$\frac{\text{Profit after tax (PaT) £}}{\text{Percentage}} \quad = \quad \frac{£2,000,000}{72\%} \quad = \quad £2,777,777 \text{ PbT}$$

The difference between the two is £777,777, which equals 28% of the PbT figure. To check it out (right side up this time):

	£	%
Profit before tax (PbT)	2,777,777	100.0
Less tax	(777,777)	(28.0)
Profit after tax (PaT)	2,000,000	72.0

Here's an exercise to try using this method:

Exercise 5.3

Capital investment	£4,900,000
Profit required (after tax)	20%
Corporation tax	28%
Fixed costs	£600,000
Administration costs	£435,000
F&B & other dept profit	£200,000
Rooms expenses/room	£20.30
Available rooms/day	76
Occupancy per year	70%

What room rate needs to be charged to achieve the required return on investment for a year?

Rooms available

Rooms sold (available × occupancy %)

(£)

Profit required (after tax) (Capital investment × profit %)

Add back tax (gross up) = Profit before tax

Add back fixed costs

Add back administration costs

= Departmental op. profit

Less F&B and other departmental profits

= Rooms profit

Add back rooms expenses (rooms sold × amount per room)

= Rooms revenue required

= Average room rate required (revenue divided by rooms sold)

Rate plus VAT (multiply by 1.2)

Activity

Are there any new projects you can identify (in your business, in your area or mentioned in the press) where you think this method might be used? Could you use it for pricing where you're not changing the physical building, say for a new product range?

Marketer's method of pricing

The accountant's methods of pricing only use costs and profits – they don't take into account any market conditions. The price may generate a profit – but will the customer pay it?

Market-based pricing takes the approach that it is the customer that decides the price, depending on the availability of the product, the local economy, competition and so on. Most of the time the pricing is fairly realistic, and does cover the costs, but this may not always be the case. You can see this in action in the supermarkets – compare the price of a tin of baked beans or a loaf of bread. You may find a very low price indeed, particularly of a 'value' own-brand product which can in no way cover all the costs. This is a deliberate ploy to attract you to that branch, and to persuade you to buy their other products as well, which do generate lots of profits. It's called loss leadership.

Competition

In general, the greater the competition, the lower the prices you will find. If there isn't competition, prices tend to be high. If you compare the price of a flight from Heathrow to Boston (lots of competition) and one to Aberdeen (very little competition) you'll see that you pay about double the price for about eight times the distance.

In hospitality and tourism, market-based pricing depends on both the season (think about package holiday prices in August against those of September) and on the location and product. For instance, a lodge-style hotel will need to be competitive with other similar businesses in the area, unless they have some unique selling point which gives them the opportunity to charge a premium price. Similarly a leisure centre may be competing with other facilities for exercise classes, children's parties, group swimming lessons, local authority contracts and so on.

Another example might be a pizza restaurant. An independent restaurant would look at the prices being charged by other, similar, businesses in the area and then price themselves either the same or marginally cheaper. However, big chains look at their competition nationally rather than locally – hence the similarity of prices between the major players all around the country. Their prices, therefore, have a national influence rather than a local one.

No obvious competition?

Market-based pricing is also used even where there is no immediate obvious competitor – perhaps simply to attract customers at all. A pub in a village may have to offer good affordable food, special beer and a wide-screen TV with cable-network football if it is to compete against a can of supermarket beer, a ready-meal and home TV.

Activity	Look in your local area for prices of different hospitality or tourism products such as coffee shops, take-away sandwiches, chips, bed-and-breakfast or pub beer. Compare the prices for similar products. If one place charges higher prices can you identify why? Is the product worth the higher price? Do the customers get value for money?

Fitting the methods together

If you are to get the best result from both the market price and the costs you need to look at both together. One approach is to cut the costs a little to match the reduced price so that at least break-even and if possible a profit is made – it is called backward pricing. This means taking both proposed prices – the market price and the cost-based price, and then cutting the costs without affecting the quality of the product or service, too much.

Suppose you were a hotel reservation manager quoting for a tour group who require a room and breakfast for two nights, for 60 rooms – a sizeable group for which you have space but whom you know are looking for a very competitive price. Your normal costs are, per room, per night:

	(£)
Room labour	11.50
Room linen	5.00
Guest supplies	1.00
Other costs	2.00
Breakfast	9.00
Total	28.50

You would normally require a 65% contribution on this booking so the rate would be:

$$\frac{\text{Variable costs £}}{\text{Cost \%}} = \frac{£28.50}{35\%} = £81.43 \text{ per room night}$$

But this is too high – they say they won't pay more than £65. Suppose you normally change the sheets and towels every day, but for this group were to only change them on departure. This would cut the linen costs to £2.00 per room (a £3 saving) and also the labour costs by another pound. The figures would then be:

$$\frac{\text{Variable costs £}}{\text{Cost \%}} = \frac{£24.50}{35\%} = £70.00 \text{ per room night}$$

This is still a bit high, but you could then consider whether there would be any additional revenue from this group. If you could persuade them to eat dinner in the restaurant, generating more profit (especially if they could eat at 18.30 when you are normally quiet) then you could consider offering the £65 rate which would give you a 62.3% contribution (£65.00 less £24.50= £40.50 contribution).

The last factor to consider is what would happen if you *didn't* take this booking. Would you be able to sell all the rooms – and at what rate? Is it better to take this booking or can you risk having empty rooms?

Quality

You always need to ensure that the quality of the product is maintained. In the above example you were actually cutting the service but you can assume that the tour group wouldn't be comparing notes with other guests as to whether their beds were changed and other guests were not. It's not acceptable to cut standards where they are visible – say by offering a sub-standard meal.

Activity Think about times when you've been offered the same product as some-one else – but paid a higher rate for it (e.g. a cut-price airline or train ticket). How did you feel?

Offering discounts

Discounting means lowering prices for a short period of time. Again you can see the supermarkets doing it by offering two pounds off a bottle of wine, or 'buy-one-get-second-half-price'. This is done for two main reasons:

☐ As a loss leader, which we've mentioned earlier

☐ To attract customers at a time of low volumes so as to cover some of the fixed (as well as variable) costs.

The important point here is that you offer a discount *off* a price – not reduce the price permanently. This means that the price can go back to normal at the end of the promotion without customers getting upset.

The accounting view of pricing would say that you always must charge a price to cover variable costs so you can't discount down below the cost price. You may want to change your method of service, or portion size, to ensure that costs are reduced too. Marketing people say that, as long as sales in other areas will compensate, you can go as low as you wish.

How much can I discount?

Figure 5.3: Discounting

Level	Product A Low fixed costs	Product B High fixed costs
£7.00 Selling price	£1.00 Profit	£1.00 Profit
£6.00	£1.00 Fixed Costs	£4.00 Fixed Costs
£5.00		
	£5.00 Variable costs	
£2.00		£2.00 Variable costs

What does this mean?

☐ £7.00 is the normal selling price for both products. Product A has a high proportion of variable costs, and a low proportion of fixed costs, whereas product B is the opposite. Both generate the same profit.

☐ If you discount by 99p to £6.01 then you still make 1p profit on either product

☐ If you discount by £1.99 down to £5.01:

■ Product A – cover all variable costs, make 1p contribution to paying fixed costs

■ Product B – cover all variable costs, make £2.99 contribution to fixed costs

☐ If you discount by £4.99 down to £2.01:

■ Product A – is not viable as not covering all variable costs

■ Product B – still covers all variable costs, makes 1p contribution to fixed costs

So – for A (low fixed cost product) you can only discount down to £5.00 to ensure you cover all variable costs

For B (high fixed cost product) you can discount down to £2.00 and still cover all variable costs

Activity	Think of a range of discounts you've seen offered recently – in the supermarket, a restaurant, a clothes shop, a hotel or perhaps an electrical supplier. Can you identify *why* the discount was offered? Would the reduced prices still cover costs or are there conditions attached which actually make you spend money elsewhere in the establishment? Would this technique work in your business?

Other factors to consider

Price and volume

Think about the relationship of price to volume as higher prices may put people off, and vice-versa. Are you happy with more people – can you cope with them? If volume reduces, would this affect your staffing plans?

Covering fixed costs

At certain times (of day, of year) you may also need to attract customers rather than focusing on average spend. This is because the fixed costs have to be paid for and any contribution is better than none.

For instance a theme park will cut its prices substantially off-season (and mid-week) when there is far less demand, just to attract visitors. Once there you are 'captured' and might then buy a meal and probably something from the shop – all with high profit margins. Restaurants offer special, fixed-price menus for the same reason – and also hope that you will return one evening for a more expensive meal.

Value for money

This is as important for a five-star as a one-star product. At the lower levels the perception is that you 'get what you pay for' – but you still need your offering to be good, albeit at a limited-service level. You want to keep your customers, not frighten them away. At the 'five-star' end of the market price is also seen as an indicator of the quality – the higher the price the higher the standard of product and service the customers will expect. If you are in this environment – do you offer perceived value for money?

The perception of value for money can vary for the same person in different scenarios. A business customer may have totally different expectations when on an expense account as opposed to spending their own money. You yourself may react differently in an expensive pub compared to a cheaper one or even if you are on holiday as opposed to going out after work. It's all about expectation, and managers need to make sure they offer the customer what they expect, or better.

Price sensitivity

This means how easy or how difficult it is to change prices – and different sectors, and products, react differently here. Five-star and first-class services are not price sensitive – customers are unlikely to object to minor changes. However, high-street fast food chains are very price sensitive, customers reacting instantly and changing to another provider if the price is increased more than considered reasonable. Even where there is a captive market, for instance on a train, customers may opt not to buy (or bring their own supplies) if the product is considered too expensive.

Price elasticity

This recognises that the demand for products and services may vary – which can affect the price to be charged. For example, where there is a single resort complex the guests have little choice as to where they will eat – they have to stay within it and accept the prices charged. Similarly students on-campus will also have only a limited choice if they wish to buy a hot meal. This is 'inelastic demand' – there is little competition except between outlets of the same business. Elastic demand is where customers can choose from a range of outlets run by different operators – in towns there are many different pubs all offering similar products and styles, all in competition with each other for your custom.

Non-profit organisations

Are your prices market-driven or even commercial? They may be determined by some other factor, such as local authority regulations (e.g. school meals) or by union negotiation (as in a factory staff eating facility). As a result, even within the food-service sector, there may be different types of prices and hence different cost percentages. For contract catering, for example, prices may be low to keep the customers on-site for a short lunch break. The cost percentage may be very high as the company being serviced may pay for most of the additional costs such as payroll.

Activity How are prices determined in your organisation? Are there different prices for the same product at different times? Are different methods used for different products? What about your meals, if you have them – how are they priced or costed?

Package pricing

We've looked at the different methods of pricing individual items and also quoting for a small group where only two elements are taken into account (room and breakfast) but you may also need to put together a single price which includes a range of items. The benefit of this to the customer is that they gain 'one-stop-shopping' – all the elements they need are grouped together in a single price and normally at a discount. For the operator there is also a benefit – only one price to charge the customer per item, not lots of separate charges, and so less cost in administration, stationery (for printing bills) and so on – and less likelihood of mistakes and queries.

Packages can be put together for all types of offers – a hotel weekend break, a conference centre package, a day trip to a theme park. They can be very low prices (food plus drink plus a game of bowls, for instance) to enormously expensive such as a fully-inclusive round the world cruise.

The usual approach is to add the *selling prices* of all the different elements together and then apply some level of discount – but how much to give? Again this may depend on the time of year and how much you need the business to fill spare capacity (unused rooms, restaurant or airline seats are wasted if not used on the day – so any sale is better than none). At this point you can look at the costs for the different elements and, as long as they are all covered, you can quote a price somewhere between the cost price and the full selling price. The more you want the business, the more discount you are able to give.

Discounting package prices

There is a great deal more flexibility in a hotel or airline for changing package prices than there are in other sectors where the cost structures are different (see Chapter 4). Managers need to know that they cannot discount as much in a restaurant or tour package, for instance, as they can in a hotel or on a flight.

Here are two examples of a package – one for a conference in a hotel, the other a one-day tour to a city, including entrance to a museum. The prices for the individual items are the average prices charged to customers in the departments for these – for instance, breakfast is the normal menu price.

Conference		One-day tour	
Item	Price (£)	Item	Price (£)
Accommodation (2 nights)	160	Hire of coach	25
Breakfasts (2)	30	Driver	10
Buffet dinner	30	Courier/guide	10
Gala dinner	60	Entrance fees	20
Lunch (2)	40	Coffee break	5
Coffee/tea breaks (4)	10	Lunch	20
Meeting room hire	30		
Equipment hire	20		
Stationery/conference pack	10		
Total	390	Total	90

Which is the more flexible in terms of discounting? If you look back to the earlier chapters where we discussed profit margins you'll see that the accommodation area has the highest margins – and so the highest opportunity for discounts (hence the conference is more flexible on pricing).

Activity   Look at a holiday brochure which allows a customer to put their own package price together (say a flight or ferry plus villa hire) and compare the prices for high season and low season. See if you can work out which are the most price-sensitive elements – that is, those that are discounted the most.

The need for information

This is crucial to the exercise! There's no point in trying to find the optimum price if you don't know all your costs. Managers need to have information about the market as well so that you know both 'sides' of the pricing argument – the accountant's and the marketer's information. This will ensure that you can make the best-informed decision which will (hopefully) satisfy the need for revenue and the need for profit (or covering the costs).

Breaking even

The last section of this chapter uses cost behaviour to work out how many of a product or service you need to sell in order to cover all your costs – in other words, to reach *break-even point* (BEP). After this point is reached then you can start to make a profit from all the extra items you sell.

To work out a BEP you need first to find the *contribution margin* (CM). To do this you need to:

1. Split your costs into fixed and variable

2. Work out the total variable cost per customer or item sold

3. Find the price per customer or item

Then you can work out your CM. This takes the variable costs (those directly incurred by selling the item) and subtracts them from the selling price. It's usually expressed as a formula:

CM = Sales minus variable costs

The most common (and understandable) approach is to show it for a single unit or item. Here's an example:

	(£)
Selling price	8.00
Variable costs	(3.20)
Contribution margin	4.80

Break-even point

Now you can work out the BEP. You could do this longhand but the simplest way is to use a formula. This takes the total fixed costs and divides them by the CM, preferably the CM per unit, so the formula is:

$$\text{Break Even Point} = \frac{\text{Fixed costs £}}{\text{Contribution margin/unit £p}}$$

This gives you the BEP in units, which is the point at which all costs have been paid for (fixed and variable).

Here's an example using the CM shown above. If the total fixed costs are £6,000 then the calculation is:

$$\text{Break-even point} = \frac{\text{Fixed costs £}}{\text{Contribution margin/unit £p}} = \frac{£6,000}{£4.80} = 1,250 \text{ units}$$

To cover all the costs you need to sell 1,250 units at a selling price of £8.00 each. Alternatively, you can work out the total in sales revenue (money) and for this you use the contribution margin percentage, rather than the amount per unit. The CM% for the above would be:

	(£)	(%)
Selling price	8.00	100.0
Variable costs	(3.20)	(40.0)
Contribution margin	4.80	60.0

Using the same BEP formula:

$$\text{Break-even point} = \frac{\text{Fixed costs £}}{\text{CM \%}} = \frac{£6,000}{60.0\%} = £10,000 \text{ (sales)}$$

Check it back to see if it works – 1,250 units at £8.00 each equals £10,000 of sales.

BEP for profit

This process can also be used to calculate how many you need to sell to make a profit. What you do is add on the profit required to the fixed costs – and the rest of the formula is the same.

$$\text{Break-even point} + \text{Profit} = \frac{\text{Fixed costs £} + \text{Profit £ required}}{\text{Contribution margin/unit £}}$$

Using the same CM and fixed costs as before, how many do you need to sell to make a profit of £1,200?

$$\text{Break-even point} + \text{Profit} = \frac{\text{Fixed costs £} + \text{Profit £ required}}{\text{Contribution margin/unit £p}} = \frac{£6,000 + £1,200}{£4.80} = 1,500 \text{ units}$$

To prove the BEP + Profit works then you could check it back by calculating the P&L using 1,500 as the number of items sold.

	Total (£)	Per cover (£)	(%)
Sales (1,500 × £8.00)	12,000	8.00	100.0
Variable costs	(4,800)	(3.20)	(40.0)
Contribution margin	7,200	4.80	60.0
Fixed costs	(6,000)		
Profit	1,200		

Break-even charts

You could use a break-even chart to compare your pricing strategies. Line-charts are covered in Chapter 9. If you first plot the costs then you can plot the sales at different unit selling prices – say three different levels. Then you can find the BEP of each on the chart and compare them – and the profits.

Exercise 5.4: London restaurant company

Here's an exercise to practise BEP. A restaurant company in London is planning to open a large new restaurant in an old warehouse open every day of the year. A return on investment (profit) of 15% is required. The first year's budget is:

Average spend	£43.00	
Cost of sales	32%	
Other variable costs	15%	(which includes some labour)
Salaries	£750,000	
Rent and rates	£700,000	
Insurance	£80,000	
Administration	£120,000	

Furniture and equipment will cost £4,500,000 and is to be depreciated over 10 years.

You are asked to:

☐ Calculate the number of covers required per year for the restaurant to break even

☐ Calculate the number of covers required per year for the restaurant to achieve the required return.

And here's another exercise to practise both pricing and BEP together:

Exercise 5.5: Farm park offer

A small farm park is looking to increase its number of visitors and revenues. One concern is that most groups typically bring their own packed lunch and so food sales are fairly low. The owners are considering offering a special rate to groups, which would include entrance to the farm park, a packed lunch and a small souvenir, for the months of June, July and August. The existing business shows the following results for a month and will not be affected by the new package.

	per month
Visitors	6,500
Variable wages	£4,000
Variable expenses	£890
Variable overhead	£1,750
Fixed costs per year are	£220,000
Profit % required	30%
Average entrance fee	£5.50

The variable costs per visitor for the special offer are expected to be the same as normal except for additional variable costs of £3.25 for the lunch and souvenir. Other costs for the package are a total of £1,700 for the initial promotion and advertising for the three-month season. The expected visitors for the package are an average of 40 for each of the 8 weekend days each month, and 25 for each of the weekdays.

Can you:

☐ Work out the selling price per visitor for the package to achieve the required profit margin

☐ Work out the number of visitors needed for the package to break even

☐ Find the profit from the existing and new business.

Tip   The cost of the advertising needs to be split between all the estimated new visitors to find out the true gain from this extra business. You'll also need to work out the total variable cost per existing visitor.

Summary

We've now reached the end of the fifth chapter that has looked at pricing and break-even points. You have learned

- Different approaches to pricing – the accountant's methods and the marketer's methods
- How to calculate a price from costs to achieve a standard gross profit
- How to calculate a price for a new project, based on the investment required
- The marketing approach to pricing
- What the relevance of contribution is to pricing
- How to calculate how many products or services you need to sell to cover all your costs (break-even point) and then to make a profit.

6 Forecasting

- Why bother?
- What is it?
- Forecasting new products
- Budgets
- Strategic planning
- Forecasting cash

Introduction

Within every business there's a need to plan ahead. If we didn't then there's a likelihood of not having enough food to cook, not enough staff to serve or lots of empty rooms. You could also have too many staff, or too much food, which would lead to wastage and unnecessary expense.

Forecasting is a simple technique that lets any manager plan for the more efficient working of their area, and use of resources. Generally forecasting means to 'look ahead' but in hospitality we use it to mean planning on a short-term basis – that is: tomorrow, next week, next month. The term 'budget' is used to mean a formal, detailed plan for the next financial year and a 'strategic plan' is used for long-term (around five years) planning. We will look at these two briefly towards the end of this chapter but the main purpose is to look at forecasting and to see the effect of not planning ahead from both customer service and financial aspects. We'll also look at predicting cash flows, which helps the business manage their working capital.

By the end of this chapter, therefore, you will be able to:

- Understand the importance of forecasting to the business
- Calculate profits from forecasted volumes
- Differentiate between budgeting and strategic planning
- Calculate a cash forecast.

Why bother?

First of all let us consider the impact of *not* forecasting how many rooms in your guesthouse you will sell next Saturday night.

If you don't know how many guests you'll have:

☐ You won't be able to sell the empty rooms (losing revenue)

☐ You won't know how many sausages, or how much bread to order

☐ You won't know how many clean sheets and towels you will need

☐ You won't know how many staff to call in on Sunday morning to serve breakfast and clean the rooms.

Of course, you could order the same as you always do but that might cause wastage of food and have your staff standing around doing nothing – or run out of food and have the staff unhappy because they're overworked (and also unhappy customers who might not return).

Here's another example. If you run a theme park and don't forecast visitors for a Wednesday in autumn, term time, you could keep all your outlets open, resulting in:

☐ Over-staffing

☐ Wasting food that doesn't get purchased and wasting electricity

☐ Upsetting customers because the food looks stale and the staff look unmotivated

☐ A loss of money as a result.

For cost sector and other types of catering (such as in hospitals and inflight catering) forecasting can be even more important as margins are so tight – if they don't forecast accurately there could be wastage which could mean the difference between break-even and a loss situation. So you can see that whatever the size and type of operation, planning is important for everybody – and not just to save money.

What is forecasting?

Forecasting is usually a short-term prediction of levels of trade, and so is more accurate than a budget that was probably prepared months ago. It's often more realistic – what we are likely to do rather than what we hope might happen. The approach tends to be more simple than a budget and may just be a prediction of volume (rooms, covers, visitors) to assist with staffing and ordering, or to identify gaps where an extra push on sales is required. So, a forecast allows planning of:

☐ Selling strategy

☐ Staffing (ratio of fixed headcount and casuals, or using up of holidays)

☐ Maximisation of occupancy and rate

☐ Open/closure policy for outlets

☐ Purchasing and storage (particularly perishable products)

☐ Cash flow.

How it works

Let's look at the process – see Figure 6.1:

The forecast starts with the revenue management system which forecasts the rooms sold, and hence the sleepers (customers).

Rooms and sleepers information goes to:

☐ Reception and porters – for staffing levels at check in/out

☐ Housekeeping – for cleaning rooms and linen stocks

Figure 6.1: Forecast flow chart for a leisure hotel (the most complex type of structure).

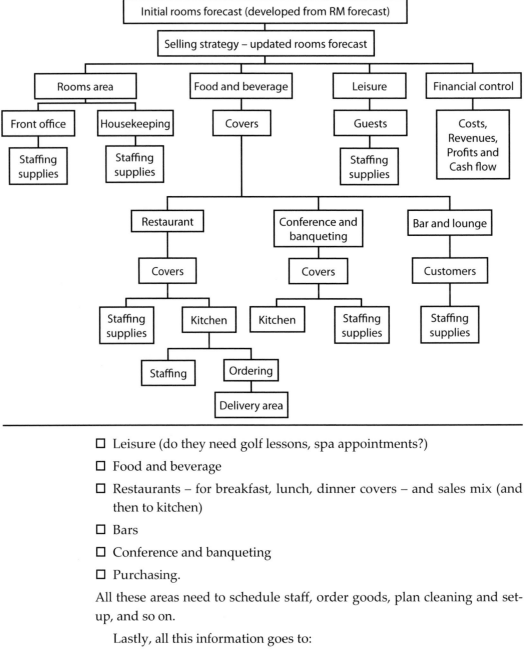

- ☐ Leisure (do they need golf lessons, spa appointments?)
- ☐ Food and beverage
- ☐ Restaurants – for breakfast, lunch, dinner covers – and sales mix (and then to kitchen)
- ☐ Bars
- ☐ Conference and banqueting
- ☐ Purchasing.

All these areas need to schedule staff, order goods, plan cleaning and set-up, and so on.

Lastly, all this information goes to:

- ☐ Financial control – for planning cash flows and profit forecasts

Other sectors are, in theory, not so complex but may well be more difficult in practice. In hospitals, for instance, most of the cleaning is routine so not affected by volumes. Catering 'only' relies on staff numbers (probably fairly stable), visitors (probably similar) and patients. But – how do you predict the number of patients, and what they will be able to, or like to eat? Since food is important to recovery you would want to give patients food to tempt their appetite, but on a very limited budget you don't have scope for wastage. You will have to rely on experience, past trends and asking patients to order in advance.

So – we need to forecast:

Daily – 'do we have spare tables we need to fill tonight?' 'Do I need an extra room attendant?' 'How many bread rolls should I order for tomorrow?'

Weekly – 'if next week's quiet we could use up some spare holiday days that are owing'.

Monthly – 'do we need to offer a discounted rate on our rooms next month?'

Seasonally – 'there's a new tourist bus running in the summer. Can I promote my attraction to these extra visitors?'

Why do we forecast?

To enable managers to plan, and staff to work, more effectively.

Mini-case

A hotel chef considered himself to be an artist, not an accountant, so he ordered what he pleased. He couldn't be bothered with looking at forecasts of sleepers so he could estimate how many croissants he would need each morning – so he had a standard order. The result was:

- Some days there weren't enough croissants for the customers – equals unhappy customers

- Other days there were too many croissants so the staff had to eat Croissant Pudding (a version of bread-and-butter pudding) for lunch (again!) – equals unhappy staff.

Timing

Forecasting is done on a daily (perhaps by meal period), weekly or monthly basis particularly where business volumes are very changeable. If demand is stable and constant (residential care, long-stay hospitals, prisons, army catering) then you may think that forecasting isn't relevant. However,

Forecasting

people have likes and dislikes and so you may still need to predict the menu-mix for ordering and production. You will see the effect if we look at a few examples.

A small visitor attraction

Next week's projected visitors

Day	Number
Monday	400
Tuesday	400
Wednesday	600
Thursday	800
Friday	1,200
Saturday	2,000
Sunday	2,200

Let's look at consumption: 40% will bring their own food (and sit in the picnic area, which will need cleaning); the rest will eat lunch in the outlets – half in the cafe, 10% in the restaurant and the rest from the takeaway (which also means mess in the picnic area). Half of all visitors will also eat ice creams (the weather is forecast to be very hot).

Day	Projected visitors	Own food	Eat lunch	Cafe	Restaurant	Takeaway	Ice cream
		40%	60%	50% of those eating lunch	10% eating lunch	40% eating lunch	50% total
Monday	400	160	240	120	24	96	200
Tuesday	400	160	240	120	24	96	200
Wednesday	600	240	360	180	36	144	300
Thursday	800	320	480	240	48	192	400
Friday	1,200	480	720	360	72	288	600
Saturday	2,000	800	1,200	600	120	480	1,000
Sunday	2,200	880	1,320	660	132	528	1,100

In addition to the permanent staff, casual workers are needed. Extra staffing is based on one person per 200 visitors.

Day	Projected visitors	Casual staff
Monday	400	2
Tuesday	400	2
Wednesday	600	3
Thursday	800	4
Friday	1,200	6
Saturday	2,000	10
Sunday	2,200	11

You now have predictions for both the catering outlets and staffing in terms of volume so you can plan your ordering. The same could be done for the shop although the number of items on sale will be greater, and they won't be perishable in the same way as food eaten on the day. It doesn't matter too much – unless it's nearing the end of the season – if you have too many postcards, key-rings and cuddly toys in stock.

In-flight catering

Flights for tomorrow ('economy' class only):

Destination	Paris	New York	Hong Kong
Snack	300		
Lunch		400	
Dinner			350
Breakfast			350

You normally allow 10% vegetarian – which should have pre-ordered when the flight was booked, but isn't always. Of the rest, the main meals are usually split equally between a meat and a fish dish (breakfast is split into meat or egg), to allow for dietary needs and taste. You also need to allow an extra 5% for staff food for the long-haul flights only (the Paris flight is so short the airline staff don't have time to stop for a break).

The Paris flight is easy – snacks are all the same and suitable for vegetarians, so the ordering and production planning is straightforward. The long-haul flights are a little more complex.

	New York	Hong Kong		
	Lunch	Dinner	Breakfast	Total economy
Meals for passengers	400	350	350	700
Add 5% staff = total meals	420	368	368	736
Vegetarian 10%	42	36	36	72
Meat 50% of the rest	189	166	166	332
Fish 50% of rest	189	166		166
Egg 50% of rest			166	166

You would now need to add on the business and first class passengers, who have different menus entirely.

Hotel staffing

A small hotel needs to consider how many staff it needs in addition to its core workforce. The action might be:

	Occupancy	Staffing
October	70%	1 extra required
November	80%	2 extra required
December	60%	Normal staff will cover
January	45%	Use up bank holidays and days owing

Activity   Think of a fast-food outlet. What do they need to forecast? How would they use this to help plan staffing? Remember back to the flexible work-force approach and scheduling by the hour to match peaks and troughs in volumes.

Who does the forecast?

You do! If you are a manager in a unit or department then you know your business – and are the best person to estimate what's going to happen on a short-term basis. You may need information from other areas, but you should estimate realistically what the volumes are going to be.

Forecasting profits

In addition to forecasting volumes, senior managers are also interested in forecasting sales and costs. This can be kept fairly simple, using volumes, predicted average spends and the average costs per customer. Where you have fairly volatile segments then it helps to show the split of these too. This isn't just for accommodation – as we've seen other types of hospitality also have market segments. As an example, a casino can forecast different types of gamblers, split by different types of day – these are 'graveyard', 'day' and 'swing' sessions (you can work out which is which!). They forecast:

☐ How many hours are played at each game

☐ How much is bet per game and per hour

☐ What the percentage of winnings is (to the gambler and to the house).

It works for both slot machines and table games and so gives data as to how much cash is needed too (there's more on cash flow later in this chapter).

Activity   Does your department do any forecasting? If so, find out how it is done (if you're not directly involved) – what information is needed, and where this comes from. Why not then ask somebody else how their department or unit does it?

Changes in levels of business

You can also use forecasting techniques to look at the effect of changes in levels of business. Here are some figures to calculate to see the effect of a 20% rise or fall in volume. (Yes, you can use cost volume profit – BEP – methods for this too; see Chapter 5.)

Exercise 6.1: Guest house

Occupancy	Normal	Down 20%	Up 20%
Rooms sold	10		
Average rate	£80.00		
Breakfast cost per room	£5.00		
Supplies cost per room	£18.00		
Fixed costs	£210		
Totals	£	£	£
Sales	800		
Food cost	(50)		
Staff & supplies	(180)		
Fixed costs	(210)		
Profit	360		

Tip Fill in the top sections (per person figures) first. The fixed costs and the costs per room don't change. Once you've got the new volumes then you can work out the totals. You'll find the answer at the end of the book.

You can see the difference in profit for the different levels of business. These all look healthy but it might not have been so good on another day with different circumstances.

Exercise 6.2

What if the costs are predicted to change too? What would happen if they all went up by 5%? Try this too – here's the grid again.

	Occupancy normal	Occupancy down 20%, costs up 5%	Occupancy up 20%, costs up 5%
Rooms sold	10	8	12
Average rate	£80.00	£80.00	£80.00
Breakfast cost per room	£5.00		
Supplies cost per room	£18.00		
Fixed costs	£210		
Totals	£	£	£
Sales	800	640	960
Food cost	(50)		
Staff & supplies	(180)		
Fixed costs	(210)		
Profit	360		

Tip	To add 5% multiply by 1.05. Do the per-person figures first and then recalculate the totals.

Exercise 6.3

Here's a 'what if' question for you to practise.

Forecasted trade looks disappointing and the managers are trying to improve sales. They suggest that sales could be increased by 10% if they did a mailshot costing £1,000. The other possibility is spending £20,000 on new equipment that could also increase sales by £50,000. What should they do (ignore depreciation)?

Sales	£600,000
Food & beverage costs	40%
Labour costs (variable)	20%
Salaries	10%
Other costs (variable)	8%
Fixed costs	20%

Look at the answer at the end of the book. You can see that the mailshot suggestion results in an extra £60,000 of sales and the equipment £50,000 of sales. The problem is that the new sales incur additional costs. Despite this the mailshot is worth it financially, but in contrast the equipment purchase isn't – in the short-term.

However, you do need to think about the long term benefits. Will the mailshot generate a permanent increase in sales? Do you really need the new equipment anyway (for health and safety reasons, for example)? If the equipment will last a long time the cost isn't all incurred in the one year – it can be depreciated over its life span (see Chapter 2). If the equipment were to last 5 years then the cost per year would be £4,000, not £20,000, which could significantly alter the result. It's never quite as simple as it looks!

Activity	Can you see any areas in your work that could be improved by spending a small amount of money that would then either generate more sales or reduce costs? Why not put a few figures together? If they are beneficial, why not show them to your manager?

Formal forecasting methods

There are some complicated statistical (and graphical) methods of forecasting that are mentioned in many of the accounting textbooks. They use past data to plot trends and then forecast for the future, and are of particular use in Revenue Management. If you understand about regression and correlation then please read up about them – we don't cover them here.

Forecasting new products

Most of the forecasting we've discussed assumes that you've prior knowledge and lots of past data to help you. But what if you haven't? What if you have to plan from a 'zero-base'? It's then that you need a technique called Zero Based Budgeting (ZBB). If you read about it in some textbooks it can be described as a complex technique which requires looking at all aspects of an existing organisation. In hospitality we tend to have our own definition, which is for new products.

It's also a 'bottom-up' approach and requires you to decide on all aspects of your customers, their sales and costs. So, for a new hotel this can mean looking at every single market segment and 'guestimating' how many rooms you will sell (each night), what the average room rate will be and so on. For costs you have to estimate how much you will use of every single type in the period. It can take a lot of time.

> ### Mini-case
>
> A hotel had been taken over and all past records removed by the previous owners. The new managers were upgrading the facilities and so decided to do a ZBB, with instructions to calculate everything. They decided they'd gone a bit too far with this when they realised somebody had spent an hour working out how many paperclips they might use in a month. The cost of this person's salary by far outweighed the benefit of this calculation – so she moved on to more important costs. Sometimes you can overdo things a bit!

Does it work?

ZBB is obviously based on a lot of guesswork, and market research. There are plenty of examples where it hasn't worked as well as it might have. Several well-known new tourism projects have proved far less profitable than expected, because the visitor numbers just haven't achieved the levels that were estimated. Sometimes there's a political aspect to the project that means that it proceeds whereas if it were purely a commercial venture it might not.

Life span

Another factor that can influence the decision is the life of the project. If it's a one-off event that is budgeted then you also have to take the dismantling costs into account; again political considerations may outweigh the commercial aspects. There may also be a subsidy from another area that can counter-balance the losses on the hospitality section – and the four-yearly Olympics is a good example. There may be an overall loss on hospitality but this is balanced by the income from television rights and also the long-term gains to the local economy. ZBB techniques are used to calculate the costs, but the overall outcome (rather than just the financial output from hospitality) is what matters.

Budgets

Now a short explanation about budgets. If you want to read more about these then please look at the finance books on the reading list.

In hospitality a budget is a formal plan for the forthcoming financial year. It is mainly thought of as being financial but also considers how the business is performing now and what actions need to be taken to improve or maintain business levels. This could be a change of product or service, finding new markets, updating of technology and development of staff.

The main types of budget are operational (like the departmental and front-page P&Ls), capital (all the new equipment and refurbishment required) and cash. They are combined into a 'master budget'.

So, they are needed:

☐ As a plan of action

☐ To set standards and establish responsibilities

☐ For reviewing current results

☐ To assist in evaluating trends.

Methods of budgeting

The budget planning process can take many months and requires input from a range of people and sources. There are two main approaches – Top Down and Bottom Up.

Top down means that the owners decide how much money they want from their investment. They tell you what profits they expect (or the cost levels in a hospital for instance – top-down is common in the public sector). You then need to work your sales and costs to match expectations.

Bottom up means that the departments estimate what they can do and build up a budget from the estimated sales and costs, and then arrive at a profit. This approach involves all managers (and often supervisors too) so you may well be involved in the future. One of the benefits is that, by being involved, managers feel responsible for the figures that they have created and so are more likely to achieve them. This is part of responsibility accounting, which we mentioned in Chapter 2.

Not surprisingly there's often a mismatch between the 'bottom-line' figures of the two approaches, so there may be negotiation between the two 'sides' until a feasible budget is reached. This can take a lot of time.

Mini-case

The flagship property of a four-star hotel chain had spent several weeks preparing its budget in-house until the GM was happy. They took it to the Regional Director and after several changes (more sales, less costs) and another two weeks, he was happy too. Then they took it to the Finance Director, and the same happened again. Eventually a budget was arrived at that everybody was reasonably happy with (though the GM was worried about her bonus) and the budget was 'put to bed'.

One week later the chain was put up for sale and they had to do a whole new budget which showed even more profit.

How's it done?

The most common method is to use last year's figures as a basis and then build on from them, taking into account any market and business changes that are likely to have an impact in the future. If you don't have past data then you need to 'zero-base' your budget, which we discussed earlier.

Don't forget too that you are restricted in what you can do – by the space you have available, the capabilities of staff, equipment available, money for capital expenditure and so on. These are called 'limiting factors'. You can't build a new food outlet in your theme park if you don't have the space or the money, and you can't offer a new destination in your package holiday brochure if the accommodation and the flights are not available.

Forecasting

Activity   Do you get involved in the budgeting process, or is it a top-down approach? Do you know what happens to the numbers after you do them? Ask your manager if you can talk through the budgeting process in your organisation.

Strategic planning

This is long-term planning and often reviews five years ahead. Senior managers look at global and national trends and then make decisions as to future business directions. However, given the current state of political and economic uncertainty in many countries, strategic planning may be more concerned with planning possible reactions to different scenarios, rather than precise potential outcomes.

This may well affect you in the future if, for instance, they are going to expand (or contract) the business – so it's worth listening out for announcements as to future long-term plans. Expansion can mean more job opportunities whereas contraction might mean you have to do some strategic planning of your own as to when you need to find an alternative employer.

If you are thinking about opening your own business then you also need to plan strategically. When you discuss your ideas with a bank they are going to want to see:

☐ A three-year business plan. This isn't just the financial numbers (budget) but also how you are going to achieve it. Your marketing plans are as important as your financial plans. The bank wants to know how you will persuade customers to try your products or services, and how much they will spend. You will also need to plan your costs.

☐ Details of the fixed assets you need to buy, and the property if relevant

☐ A three-year cash flow forecast (which we will do shortly).

So, strategic planning isn't just for 'top managers' – it affects you too.

Forecasting cash

We'll discuss the importance of cash as part of working capital as well as how to collect (and spend) it, in the next chapter. Here we will just look at how to predict cash levels at a particular time. This technique can be adapted to suit your own finances – in other words, to predict your own bank balance.

First a reminder where cash comes from and goes to:

Cash In	Daily	Cash
		Cheques
		Credit cards (Maestro/Visa)
		Debit cards
		BACS/direct debit payments from debtors
	Monthly	Interest from banks & building societies
		Other investment income, rents and so on
Cash Out	Monthly	Payroll
		Cheques to suppliers
		BACS payments to suppliers
		Payroll taxes
	Quarterly	Value Added Tax

So each month there are days of high outgoings that can require large cash balances at the bank unless the business is careful to manage its cash.

How to calculate cash

Receipts – payments = surplus (or deficit) for the month

Surplus (or deficit) + opening cash balance* = closing cash balance

*(whether positive or negative)

But – we have to take into account the time people take to pay us and the time we take to pay our bills.

This is a simple cash flow exercise. Here are the first two months, please try to do the third month yourself. Each month consists of four weeks. To make it more straightforward we will assume that the business is just starting up and there haven't been any sales and costs before.

Sales	Month 1 = £3,500, month 2 = £7,200, month 3 = £8,000. Of these, 75% pay in cash, the rest by credit the following month
Cost of sales	40% of the sales figure, paid the following month (sometimes called 'in arrears')
Expenses	£1,400 per month, also paid in the following month
Payroll	30% of the sales figure, paid in the current month
Cash in the bank at the start ('opening cash')	£200

The best way to approach this is to do your 'workings out' *before* you try and plot when they will all be paid.

So, the process is:

1. Write down all the information you need

2. Do all the workings out

3. Draw up the table format, as below

4. Put the figures in the relevant spaces

5. Add up the totals and arrive at a bank balance (which should be the end figure on your bank statement)

Workings out

Month	1	2	3	
	(£)	(£)	(£)	
Sales	3,500	7,200	8,000	
Cash 75%	2,625	5,400		Paid in current month
Credit 25%	875	1,800		Paid following month
Cost of sales at 40% sales	1,400	2,880		Paid following month
Expenses at £1,400/month	1,400	1,400		Paid following month
Payroll at 30% of sales	1,050	2,160		Paid in current month
Opening cash balance	200			

Cash forecast for the first 2 months

	Month 1 (£)	Month 2 (£)	Outstanding
Receipts			
Cash	2,625	5,400	
Credit	0	875	£1,800 Debtors (DR)
Total	2,625	6,275	
Payments			
Cost of sales	0	1,400	£3,200 Creditors (CR)
Expenses	0	1,400	£1,400 CR
Payroll	1,050	2,160	
Total	1,050	4,960	
Surplus/deficit for period	1,575	1,315	
Opening balance	200	1,775	
Balance carried forward	1,775	3,090	

The 'outstanding' column shows how much still has to be paid – £1,800 debtors (to come in) and £4,600 creditors (to go out) so the positive bank balance hides a lot of liability.

Now it's your turn. These DRs and CRs need to be paid the following month so they've been put in the right places. You can use the spare column in the 'workings out' section above.

	Month 1 (£)	Month 2 (£)	Month 3 (£)	Outstanding
Receipts				
Cash	2,625	5,400		
Credit	0	875	1,800	
Total	2,625	6,275		

Payments			
Cost of sales	0	1,400	3,200
Expenses	0	1,400	1,400
Payroll	1,050	2,160	
Total	1,050	4,960	
Surplus/deficit for period	1,575	1,315	
Opening balance	200	1,775	
Balance carried forward	1,775	3,090	

If you had a minus figure to carry forward (a deficit) that shouldn't be a big problem if it's only for a month and you can see that you will be into surplus the next month. You just need to talk to your bank before you overdraw!

Activity

Look at your own personal cash flow and try to predict your cash coming in and going out for the next month. Then in a month's time see how accurate you were (and see if you've saved any money by being more conscious of what you were spending).

Exercise 6.4

Lastly here's another forecasting exercise to try. A departmental budget has been established with the following standard percentages:

	%
Food & beverage costs	37.0
Wages (variable)	19.5
Salaries	4.5
Fixed costs	9.0
Variable expenses	20.0
Net profit	10.0
= Total sales	100.0

After several months of trading it is apparent that the sales will only achieve a figure of £420,000, a shortfall of 20% on the budget. A forecast is required to predict the anticipated net profit, in order that remedial action may be taken where necessary.

Tip

Work out the budget sales first, and gross up, then you can work out the budget costs. Remember that fixed costs don't change – and some of those above are fixed. Once you've got the budget for them, they will stay the same amounts for the forecast.

Summary

You have now finished Chapter 6. In this chapter we considered the importance of forecasting and why it matters to business. We also looked at cash and at the difference between strategic planning, budgeting and forecasting. You have, therefore:

- Considered the importance of short-term planning within the business
- Seen what a difference a forecasted shortfall or overage can make to your profits
- Calculated variances due to shortfalls in business volumes
- Discussed the different types of business planning – forecasting, budgeting and strategic planning
- Identified areas where zero-based budgeting might be used
- Calculated cash balances.

7 Managing cash and stocks

- Cash
- Bank accounts
- Credit settlement
- Stock management

Introduction

This chapter considers the two main physical items that have potential for control problems – cash and stocks. They are part of what's known as the 'cycle of working capital'. We've seen in earlier chapters some of the ways in which these can be managed effectively but we will now concentrate on specific areas for control. First we will look at cash being both received and paid. Second, we will consider the flow of stock and the various stages at which problems can occur.

By the end of this chapter you will, therefore, be able to:

- Describe the cycle of working capital
- Identify the various stages at which cash moves in and out of the business
- Identify the various stages through which stock moves around the business
- Discuss methods of control appropriate to the operation
- Calculate ratios relevant to cash and stock control.

Cash

Cash is the 'lifeblood' of the business – without it you can't pay the bills or your staff and hence businesses can fail if they don't have enough of it. Here we will show you where the cash comes from and goes to, and how you can improve the cash flow of your business. You should note that cash is NOT the same as profits – businesses can be profitable but fail due to inadequate cash flow. We looked at forecasting this in Chapter 6.

Working capital

Cash is part of working capital, which we know from Chapter 2 is the money to run the business. As a reminder it's worked out by taking:

Current assets (CA = cash, stock, debtors, prepayments)
– Current liabilities (CL = accruals, overdrafts, creditors).

Generally speaking, if there are more CA than CL, the business is 'liquid' which means able to pay its debts. There are two ratios used to express this – the Current Ratio and Liquidity Ratio (also called the Acid Test).

$$\text{Current ratio} = \frac{\text{Current assets £}}{\text{Current liabilities £}}$$

This is expressed as an x:1 – the CA being the x and the CL being the 1. So, if you have £200 of CA and £100 of CL then the ratio (of £200:£100) is expressed as 2:1.

But – stocks take a long time to convert into cash (they have to be converted to products, sold and the cash collected) so they aren't as 'liquid' as the other CA. It's best if they are extracted before you make the comparison – if the CA without the stock is more than the CL then you're okay.

Liquidity ratio (Acid test)   = $$\frac{\text{Current assets £ – Stock £}}{\text{Current liabilities £}}$$

The 'acid test' is whether the liquidity ratio is better than 1.1:1 (as in £110:£100). If it is, then you have enough surplus of CA (without the stock) over CL to comfortably pay your bills. Even if the liquidity ratio is less than 1:1 then (although technically insolvent) it's not a disaster – you can usually borrow money assuming that it is only a short-term problem and not a long-term shortage of money.

We need to understand how money moves around the business so that we can see where it comes from and goes to. This is the 'cycle of working capital' (see Figure 7.1).

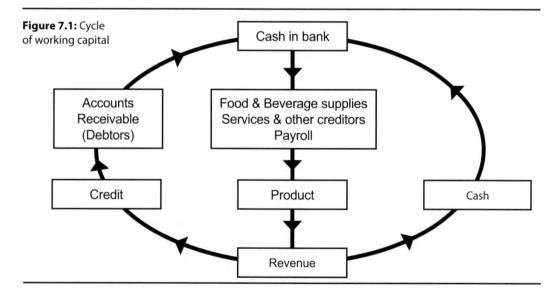

Figure 7.1: Cycle of working capital

1. First, cash is in the bank (or in floats)
2. Then it gets paid out to food and beverage and other suppliers, government agencies, utility companies (all 'accounts payable' or 'creditors'), staff (as payroll) and so on – this takes time.
3. The purchase of these produces a product or service, which is sold to generate revenue
4. The revenue is paid for by either cash, credit cards or credit account (debtors)

5. Cash sales go directly back to the bank

6. Credit cards are transacted electronically, and cash is credited to the bank account a few days later

7. Credit sales (debtors or 'accounts receivable') have to be collected (which takes time as well) until eventually they are paid which also becomes cash in the bank.

Now let's look at the different elements (excluding accruals and prepayments which we covered in Chapter 2). As with other aspects of control there are two potential problems – fraud or theft (deliberate – with cash being potentially very attractive) and errors (not deliberate and more to do with inefficiency).

Physical Cash

This comes into the operation in several different ways:

Cash from customers

☐ Sterling cash

☐ Foreign exchange

☐ Credit cards (Maestro, Visa, etc.)

☐ Debit cards

☐ Cheques

☐ Vouchers (these aren't physical cash but do have a value).

Cash from debtors

☐ Cheques

☐ Bank transfers (including credit cards)

This can also include advance deposit payments for future bookings.

Cash from interest, commission and rentals

☐ Bank and building society interest

☐ Commission on foreign exchange

☐ Direct transfers for payment of rentals (e.g. for concessions, showcases, leased car park).

Moving money

Cash should be stored in three places – the till, the safe or the bank – but of course it's not that simple, which is where the problems are likely to appear. Money has to be moved from place to place.

Customer	➜	waiting staff or receptionist, for instance
Waiting staff	➜	cashier
Cashier	➜	cash office
Cash office	➜	bank

If you receive cheques from debtors by post (as opposed to direct payment into your bank account), ideally these should be logged by a secretary or administrative assistant so that the potential for fraud is reduced.

Secretary	➜	cash office
Cash office	➜	bank

All these stages have potential for error or fraud, although the argument is that the more checks that are made the less likelihood there is for problems.

Let's consider the different types of issues that can occur with cash.

Floats

Cash floats can be small (say £100 for each of the bar staff) or enormous (£5,000 for a hotel cashier who has to make a lot of foreign exchange transactions).The usual approach is that the float is always kept at exactly the same level at the end of each shift, and any other cash received is banked whether it is correct or not. Each member of staff is responsible during their shift for their own float. When they go off duty it is either checked and signed over to a new member or staff, or it is put in the safe. If the business closes for the night then all floats should be kept in the safe – staff should never be allowed to take cash off the premises.

Activity   How safe are your floats, if you have them? Look carefully at the procedures for opening and closing safes, tills and floats. Are tills left open at night so they are obviously empty? Do two people always open the safe, and two check the cash to make sure there is no theft? Do you feel secure yourself when handling cash, or could security be improved?

Cash moving around

This can also offer opportunity for thieves so, if possible, two people should always go together – whether it's paying in to a cash office, emptying vending machines or going to the bank. It's both protection from attackers and a witness to correct procedures in case of suspicion.

Cash and stocks

> **Mini-case**
>
> Joe was responsible for 'cashing up'- at the end of the night on his own. He had to lock the takings and floats in the safe and then leave the keys in a sealed envelope ready for collection by the early duty manager.
>
> One morning the manager came on duty, opened the safe – but it was empty. Joe did not come to work that afternoon, and was never seen again. The police found out he had gone back to his home country where he could not be prosecuted.
>
> From then on the manager ensured that the cashing up and closure of the safe was witnessed, and signed for, by two people. They could still collude in a fraud, but this was far less likely now.

Cash office

Bigger businesses often have a cash office (or part of a manager's office) where the main safe is kept holding larger floats with change and petty cash. These need to be very secure both outside (lots of locks, ideally with a combination code that is changed weekly) and inside – two separate keys and a combination code. It's also sensible not to allow more than one or two staff to enter the office at any one time.

Some busy cash offices operate like banks with security windows through which the transactions are made. They may also have a night safe facility so late-working staff can deposit their takings when the cash office is closed. Security cameras are useful too.

Customers paying cash

In restaurants, making staff responsible for collecting payments from customers is one of the best incentives for accuracy, especially if they are subject to disciplinary action if they lose money. Whatever the approach, you need to have a written policy that anybody who has more than (for instance) three errors in a particular time span has to be retrained, which may mean they have a lower pay rate until they have proved they are capable again.

Walk-outs

It can be a problem stopping 'walk-outs' – if customers want to leave without paying then they will usually try to find a way somehow. This is theft, though, which eventually affects the business as a whole and so threatens your jobs. There are many scenarios where future guests expect to pay in advance (in a hotel, for a wedding reception, a theatre outing or a holiday) but this isn't feasible for an ordinary meal. All you can do is to be vigilant, take personal details if booked in advance, and try to set up physical barriers to stop people walking out.

Foreign exchange

PMS systems are programmed to accept the major currencies and will work out the rate for you, as are many EPOS systems. You do need to watch out for forged notes though (as you do with sterling) as it can be easy to 'pass off' forgeries if you are unfamiliar with a particular currency. The exchange rate you give appears less favourable than the bank rate as it includes the cost of commission that the business has to pay.

Accepting cheques

Many establishments no longer accept cheques, and it is likely they will be phased out completely within a few years. Most businesses now expect customers to use credit or charge cards, which are safer (more about these below). If your business does still accept them then this should only be in payment of goods, supported by the customer's cheque card which will guarantee up to a certain amount (it's printed on the card). You should write the details from that on to the back of the cheque (and probably swipe it through the EPOS too). Some guarantee cards also have a photo of the owner on them, so it's worth looking out for that as well. Don't forget to check that the signatures are the same too, please!

Credit and debit cards

Wherever possible, encourage the use of credit cards (Visa, Maestro, for instance) or debit cards rather than charge cards, as they are cheaper and safer. The cashier swipes the card through the till then keys in the amount of money. The customer then enters their PIN number to authorise the transaction. Not only does the system (via telephone lines back to a card provider) check that the card isn't stolen or the customer exceeded their spending limit but it also pays the cash from the operator into your bank account in the next few days.

Cash and stocks

Activity

Think about the last few times you've paid in a shop or restaurant with a credit card. Could anyone have seen you enter your PIN number – or did you just blithely key it in without noticing if anyone was close by? If someone can see your number being keyed, and then steals your card, then they can use it to spend money fraudulently. Credit card fraud is *enormous*, whether from theft of cards or by 'skimming' which is making a copy of a card and then buying items on somebody else's account.

Bank accounts

There are many different types of accounts available and it isn't part of this book to explore these. The main advice for the small business is to:

☐ Discuss terms with the bank – after all, they are borrowing your money

☐ Use current and deposit accounts, and make sure you keep the business money separate from personal money. It's also worth while keeping all the tax you have to pay (PAYE and VAT) in a separate account so you aren't tempted to use it

☐ If you have a temporary cash shortage then it may be cheaper to overdraw for one day rather than taking money out of a high-interest-bearing account.

Banking

Banking deposit slips need to be filled in by one person and ideally checked by another, unless it's your own business.

Do you bank daily? Does someone actually go to the bank or do you have a security company to collect it? Security aspects should be paramount for both cash and staff – and your costs may be partly offset by savings on insurance premiums.

If you do visit the bank, you should change the time and route you take, as even small amounts of cash can be tempting to thieves (it only takes a few snatches of a couple of thousand to build up to a nice holiday fund).

Reconciling cash

Once banked you need to reconcile the amounts to the revenue figures. There's actually a three-way check:

Cash recorded via EPOS or PMS ➜ Cash received by staff ➜ Cash banked.

Once the bank statement is received (preferably on-line so you can check immediately) then you need to check that too. Ideally they all tally – if they don't, then you need to see where the differences are and who is responsible for the shortage or overage.

Credit settlement

Types of credit settlement are credit account (account to company) or charge card (American Express, Diners and similar) for which similar processes apply as with credit cards (above), except that it may take a bit longer to gain payment. Another type of short-term credit is hotel guests signing items to their room accounts. Here it's important that staff are trained to check key cards, for signatures as well as room numbers, to ensure that the charge is made to the correct account.

Mini-case

One accounts clerk at head office reconciled all the bank statements of a company. He seemed to be a very conscientious worker, rarely took holiday and insisted that (if he were away) nobody else should do his job – he would catch up when he returned. All seemed fine until one day he was suddenly taken seriously ill.

Senior managers appointed a replacement clerk who found that money had been siphoned out of bank accounts into the absent clerk's own account where it earned a vast amount of interest. A couple of months later the money was returned so that the accounts could be balanced.

If more than one person had checked the statements then this should not have happened.

Credit accounts

'Credit is a privilege not a right'

There is often a conflict between:

Sales staff
(rooms, meals, conferences, etc.)   Versus   Credit control staff
who see success in terms of customers   who see success in terms of cash in the bank

Effective collection is dependent upon:

Before the event

☐ Applicants for credit being fully vetted (you can do this on-line, in minutes) with full credit and bank references

☐ Agreements being signed with strict credit terms

☐ Staff who take bookings being trained not to give credit without authority.

At the event

☐ Correct and legible billing (prices, number of customers) and correct documentation (vouchers, correspondence)

☐ Organiser signing off to approve bill before departure.

Invoicing

☐ Details being checked again

☐ Correct name and full address (it's surprising how many invoices can get 'lost' within a company if the exact recipient isn't specified)

☐ Timely mailing of invoices – ideally via email or electronic transfer to a named recipient.

Collection of debts

☐ Timely mailing or emailing of statements

☐ Resolution of queries

☐ Frequent and effective collection calls

☐ Insisting on direct transfers (see paying bills, below) as a condition of a contract

☐ Paying in of cheques as soon as they arrive

☐ Motivation of staff (incentives?)

☐ Commitment of all management (not just Financial Control).

Sanctions if they don't pay

☐ Use sales and marketing departments to pressure large producers

☐ Make use of any mutual contacts

☐ Threaten withdrawal of business

☐ If all else fails, don't be afraid to use professional help – a solicitor's letter can work very quickly. You can also use the Small Claims Court cheaply and efficiently to recover debts.

Measuring debtors

You can just use the 'debtors' figure on the BS but the main measure is 'debtor days'.

$$\text{Debtor days} = \frac{\text{Average debtors } £}{\text{Average daily credit sales } £} \text{ days}$$

As an example: if the debtors figure were £10,000 and the credit sales for a month (30 days) £7,500 then the calculation would be

$$\text{Average daily credit sales} = \frac{\text{Sales } £ \text{ for month}}{\text{Number of days}} = \frac{£7,500}{30} = £250 \text{ per day}$$

$$\text{Debtor days} = \frac{\text{Debtors } £}{\text{Average daily credit sales } £} = \frac{£10,000}{£250} = 40 \text{ days}$$

That means that, on average, customers are taking nearly 6 weeks to pay the credit bills to you. Since some will pay quickly (perhaps in 2 weeks), some are taking much longer. Forty days is manageable but it would help your bank balance if you could reduce this to a 30-day average.

Paying bills (creditors)

Payments are made to employees, suppliers for goods and services, statutory bodies (PAYE, VAT and so on) and local shops via petty cash.

Employees

Staff are usually paid monthly and you can't delay this as it will *immediately* affect morale and hence all aspects of the business. Most staff (including casuals) are paid through BACS (Bank Automated Clearing System) which transfers the money at a given time from your account to theirs.

Suppliers

These are paid on a regular basis that is usually monthly although sometimes you may agree specific short payment terms in exchange for cheaper prices. Services (utilities, telephone) often specify payment within two or three weeks, and perhaps via direct transfer. Many businesses now pay via bank transfer on an agreed date, saving administrative costs.

Statutory bodies

VAT and tax authorities have fixed payment terms that you can't afford to ignore as the fines can be very large and are rigidly enforced. They may also close you down if you persistently default on payments (and in the event of liquidation they claim their cash before anybody else).

Petty cash

This is a small float kept in the business for you to use in emergencies or where it's not worth ordering from a supplier. For instance, if you only want one packet of envelopes then it will be easier (and perhaps cheaper) to use petty cash to buy from the local stationers, rather than placing an order.

Helping cash flow

☐ Hold back supplier payments if you can *but* don't jeopardise goodwill or future deliveries.

☐ Delay tax payments until the last possible date

☐ Use BACS or CHAPS (similar to BACS) to pay bills as late as possible

☐ See whether it's worth taking the discounts offered by suppliers for quick payment.

and don't use that old favourite 'the cheque's in the mail' too often!

E-pay

We've already mentioned BACS which has been available for many years now. The trend is for fully automated electronic payments – or 'e-pay'. It's part of the entire business-to-business (B2B) and business-to-customer (B2C) revolution that's taking place – and by the time you read this it will already have moved on further. E-pay allows links between customer, business and bank. Simply stated it works like this:

1. You approve a supplier invoice for payment on your computer
2. Your computer system tells the bank computer system to pay £X on a specific date
3. The bank computer pays the cash from your bank account to the supplier bank account
4. It tells the supplier and your computer system that this has happened
5. Documentation is produced as evidence that the invoice is settled.

Measuring how long it takes to pay your bills

We use a similar calculation to debtors – this time it's creditor days.

$$\text{Creditor days} = \frac{\text{Average creditors £}}{\text{Average daily purchases £}} \text{ days}$$

An example

Purchases for 30 days are £24,000 and the creditor figure is £44,000

$$\text{Average daily credit purchases} = \frac{\text{Purchases £ for month}}{\text{Number of days}} = \frac{£24,000}{30} = £800 \text{ per day}$$

$$\text{Creditor days} = \frac{\text{Creditors £}}{\text{Average daily purchases £}} = \frac{£44,000}{£800} = 55 \text{ days}$$

Your suppliers are probably *not* very happy at waiting so long for payment. You need to take some action or they'll refuse to do business with you.

Stock management

We have mentioned stock control before as being closely linked to cost control and to standard costing. Here we will be looking at the processes involved in the conversion of a raw material to an item for sale – ordering, delivery, storage and issue to departments. There is more about production and usage in the standard costing (Chapter 8) and ratios were discussed in Chapter 4 on cost control. The processes are particularly designed for food and beverage although there is application for any other items that are ordered by the unit. Figure 7.2 is a flow chart of the processes.

Figure 7.2: Stock flow chart

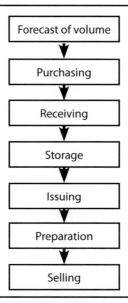

A couple of overall points about stock control. First, you need to set up systems that are safe and secure so the potential for fraud or wastage is limited. Second, you can't do everything, so you need to minimise the opportunities. If you don't spot problems early, whatever they are, then they will just get worse. In hospitality, too, you can have hundreds of stock items that aren't used very often and these are not really worth spending too much time on. It's the big things you really need to concentrate on.

Stock Items

Let's look at the type of stock items you find in hospitality and tourism. They are generally divided into two categories, perishable and non-perishable.

Perishable

These are mainly foodstuffs but some beverage has a short lifespan too. They need to have a fast turnover in order to maintain their quality. Low levels of stock are possible with daily deliveries – which is usual in large cities but may be less common in rural areas.

You need to keep minimum stocks so that freshness is maintained, but without compromising on customer service. Some sectors have converted to longer-life products (packaged or frozen) to reduce loss and help with portion control.

Non-perishable

These tend to have larger holdings as deliveries are generally less frequent.

Liquor may have a large number of stock items, depending on the type of operation and the length of the wine list. These stocks are often valuable and hence desirable to would-be thieves.

Supplies includes a range of departmental and administrative expenses – guest supplies, paper goods, cleaning materials, printed items.

Plant includes china, glass and cutlery and sometimes repairs and maintenance items.

Purchasing

Suppliers

One of the best ways of reducing the cost of what you buy is to 'shop around' for discounts on what you buy. This isn't possible for everybody, though, because you may be 'tied in' to buying from nominated suppliers, such as beverage from the brewery. Larger organisations (hospital trust, contract caterers, hotel and leisure groups) almost always have a head office purchasing department, which can negotiate discounted prices from approved suppliers, which may be the difference of profit or loss on a contract.

If you are a small local business you can choose your suppliers and there may be strong arguments for buying from other local traders. They may not be the cheapest but they should give you good service and be able to supply you at short notice if you need it. You could buy fresh produce locally but go to a 'cash and carry' warehouse to buy all your dry goods, cleaning materials and so on. For beer you can negotiate with a range of breweries and perhaps obtain discounts of up to 20% on the prices a tied house might have to pay.

Specification

It is essential to ensure that you buy the right product for the right purpose or your costs will be incorrect. This applies whether you are buying china, meat, cleaning products or new beds. You must research what you need for the job and then ideally produce a product specification that details everything. For a bunch of bananas this could include: size, number per bunch (yield), ripeness, whether fair-trade or organic, packaging, preservatives, country of origin, colour, date and time of supply as well as cost.

Large businesses such as contract caterers have very strong specifications. They will negotiate lower prices in return for guaranteed volume and quality of supply, which benefits both supplier and caterer. Smaller businesses may find it more effective to shop around for goods, although it may be better to use your energies serving your customers.

Orders

For day-to-day purchases, managers normally have authority to buy what they need, providing they are documented and that it's obvious they are not for the manager's personal consumption. For bigger, occasional purchases (unless you're a small business), you will need to complete a purchase order which will then have to be approved by senior management – and the level of authority often depends on the value of the goods. You normally should have three quotations from different suppliers to show that you have 'shopped around' for the best price.

How much to order

Order what you need! This may seem simple but many businesses just guess (remember the croissant pudding example quoted earlier). This means:

1. Looking at your stocks to see how much you have
2. Doing a forecast of what you will need until the next delivery
3. Adding a bit more 'just in case'
4. And then placing the order.

Even if you 'batch cook' – say in a food production unit – the same principles apply. There's no point in ordering things you don't need because you then have problems of storage and deterioration (and you spend cash that could be better in the bank). This is one reason why ordering from a supplier is better than going to a cash-and-carry where you may be tempted to buy more.

Cash and stocks

Activity

Think about the last time you went to a supermarket. Did you just buy what was on your shopping list, or did you add things you didn't really need? You probably do the same if you buy for work. Shopping lists are useful in business too, especially if you stick to them.

The other temptation is discounts. How many establishments have items on their shelves that they bought as a special offer – and never used?

Mini-case

A business was made an 'offer it couldn't refuse' – two cases (24 bottles in total) of what was then *the* fashionable summer drink for cocktails at a 50% discount. The problem was that fashions change. Two years later they finally realised that only 3 bottles had been used and 21 bottles were still in the cellar gathering dust. Eventually they were given to a charity for raffle prizes.

There is a formula approach to ordering called the 'economic order quantity' – you can read it up in textbooks if you want to (see the list at the end of the book). It's okay if you're in a manufacturing environment (which some catering businesses obviously are) but it's a bit cumbersome for day-to-day use.

Systems

There are lots of computerised stock control systems available now which will often also produce orders for you. It takes the stock levels held (about which more below), you add your forecast information and then it produces an order. With some systems, the computer will then e-mail the order through to the supplier for you. This is good in theory and works well for dry goods but is less successful when dealing with some fresh food. Perhaps today you want a larger size steak or melon than yesterday, for a specific dish – it's not always easy to tell a pre-programmed computer this and persuade it to order what you want.

Some companies now use an electronic 'marketplace' approach whereby they invite suppliers to 'bid' for an order on-line. The supplier offering the best price for the specification gets the business. This can be used for daily items such as meat as well as bigger purchases (furniture, for instance).

Remember, if one person orders all your stocks that could mean they have responsibility for millions of pounds of items. So, it's essential to:

☐ Have somebody of high enough calibre and experience to do the job

☐ Accurately forecast need

☐ Negotiate contract prices and specifications if feasible

☐ Change suppliers if their service or product specification declines or they become too expensive

☐ Ensure managers know how much things cost

☐ Take advantages of discounts and rebates

☐ Minimise 'kickbacks and freebies' – you'll end up paying somehow.

Receiving

This activity is really important! The 'back door' is traditionally one of the major places where losses can occur, usually due to fraud but occasionally just carelessness. Again it's crucial to have somebody you can trust to be vigilant, honest and accurate to receive goods – if you can't do it yourself. Think of the thousands of pounds worth of stock that is delivered every year.

The overall approach is that you:

1. Arrange deliveries at suitable times (you don't want four at once)
2. Check everything physically and compare it to what is listed on the delivery note and on your copy of the order form – for both quantity and quality as per specification. Write any discrepancies on the delivery note
3. Take responsibility for the goods and then move them to a safe place
4. Date stamp (and perhaps bar-code if you have a computerised system) everything to ensure correct stock rotation
5. Make sure the driver doesn't have access to other stock
6. Enter all deliveries on the computer system (if you have one), by item and price, which will update the stock records and help calculate costs.

The checking process depends on the type of goods that are being received.

Cleaning materials	Check brand name, size, quantity and perhaps strength
Stationery	Check items, number, colour if relevant
Paper goods	Check quantity, printed logo if ordered, type
Dry goods (food)	Check type, size, quantity & that containers are sealed
Frozen food	Should be delivered in a special vehicle. Check type, size, quantity and temperature, and move immediately to freezers
Fruit and vegetables	Check all items per the standard specification – this could be all the items mentioned above for bananas. Otherwise it's size, number, ripeness, and overall quality
Meat and fish	These need really careful checking. You need to make sure that it's the correct cut, weight (per portion and total), quality, freshness, temperature. They should be delivered in refrigerated vehicles but not be frozen (they can contain a lot of water if they are) unless that's what you've ordered.
Beer kegs	Check kegs are full and have correct beer type on label and that dates are correct. Chalk them to show receipt. Check empty kegs out and hand over to drayman.
Bottled beer and soft drinks	Check all crates are full and bottles are sealed. Check out counted empties, in crates, to drayman
Tanked beer or postmix	These are delivered by 'tanker' and will be pumped directly into your storage containers. These are metered so you should check the meter before the delivery starts and again at the end. The quantity delivered then needs checking against the meters on the tanker to make sure they match.
Wines and spirits	Check by name, type, size, quantity & that containers are sealed. For wine the correct year or production. You may put coloured labels on to show they are legitimate stock. Suppliers may take away empties – if they do, check them out too.

Cash and stocks

Some items may be delivered directly to a unit – either by the delivery person or by the receiving clerk. Fresh produce often bypasses stores and goes straight to a kitchen. If this happens then the same processes need to take place.

Activity	How are things received in your operation? Are the controls watertight or do you think that some items are 'going walkabout'? If so, is there anything you can do about this?

Storage

You need to keep stock safely and securely so that it doesn't 'walk' or deteriorate. You also need to make sure that it is consumed before its 'use by' date, so stock rotation is very important.

Legal requirements

There is a lot of health and safety legislation about storing different types of products. Many need storing separately (meat separate from fish, cleaning materials apart from food, and so on) so you must check that you are following correct procedures. If you need help on this contact your local council or your professional association (see the website list at the back of the book). You also need a food hygiene certificate if handling food, and other certified training if you're handling certain chemicals or gas.

Rotation

Stock rotation generally follows the FIFO rule – 'first in first out'. This can be tricky if you're not organised in your stores, freezers or fridges. The rules are:

☐ Date stamp everything if it doesn't already have one

☐ Move old stock to the front and new stock to the back

☐ Periodically check that the stock is being used. If it isn't then you need to take action. This could mean putting on a special promotion to sell it off cheaply, asking the chef to use it up in staff meals or contacting the supplier to see if it can be returned. If you can't use it then see if a charity can take it from you. You'll have to 'write off' the value (which means it becomes a cost to the business) but at least it's not then taking up space and potentially going off.

☐ If stock does deteriorate then it needs disposing of – again there are rules (and about chemicals in particular).

Keeping stock safe can be as simple as a good lock and only two keys (one in use and one in the safe as a spare). If you have to have more keys, then they need to be signed in and out so that you always know who has access and therefore who is responsible. All the sophisticated stock systems in the world are useless if somebody can walk in and take things.

You may have many storage areas – the more outlets you have the more stores you'll have. Managers like to have their stock accessible, which helps them supply customers but can be a problem for control. Ideally you have a main stores area and then keep minimum stocks in departments.

Mini-case

Jim was a chef. He worked long hours and was a trusted member of the team. Just after he had left the premises late one evening he returned, escorted by a policeman. Jim had tripped on the pavement (perhaps having imbibed some of the kitchen brandy, but that's another story) and the policeman heard a 'clink' of metal and decided to investigate further. Not only was Jim 'borrowing' some of the cutlery belonging to the business (he was having a dinner party the following day) but he had also walked out with several kilos of prime steak.

Stock levels

For fresh food, stock levels often depend on demand – and that depends on accurate forecasting. Depending on the availability of deliveries you really only want a couple of days' worth of fresh food in your fridges and stores so you plan the ordering to ensure only minimum stocks are held. You can usually buy in fairly small quantities to match what you need.

For dry and frozen goods you often have to order by case and also might only be able to get a delivery once a week or so, so stocks can fluctuate a little. You may want to keep about two weeks' supply of these, on average. For keg and bottled beer (which can go off quite quickly) a low stock level is also advisable. Wines and spirits can usually be ordered in single bottles.

It obviously depends on location as to the availability of supply. If you're on a remote island and the boat comes once a week then you may have to have higher stock levels and different menus than if you were in the middle of the city. Cruise ships also have to keep high stock levels due to problems of supply, and negotiate for fresh food in a variety of locations.

Cash and stocks

> ### Mini-case
>
> A purchasing manager heard 'on the grapevine' that the price of coffee from South America was likely to rise substantially due to a bad crop, and so ordered several months' supply. He forgot that there are other areas in the world that also grow coffee. These had an excellent harvest and, as a result, the price of coffee actually went down. The result was that the business paid more for coffee overall than it needed to, this took an enormous amount of storage space and cash was used for buying this which could have been invested.

Par stocks

For many items you need to establish a par stock – a level of stock that is high enough to keep you supplied but low enough not to tie up space or cash.

How to calculate a par level:

1. Find out how often you can receive a delivery (say every seven days)
2. Add on the number of days between ordering and delivery (say another two)
3. Work out how many you consume in this number of days (nine in total)
4. Add a little more for a 'cushion'
5. This becomes your par level. It should be written down – often actually on the shelves where the goods are stored. If you have a computerised system then this number can be input and orders will be made based on this stock level.

At most times of year you stick to this level of stock. Whatever is used is replaced, and no more. Hence, if you use six bottles of whisky in one week, then that's what you re- order. The following week you may only use five, so you reorder five, and so on. The only time you will need to increase your order is when usage increases or when deliveries are limited (say over Christmas and New Year). If you find that you are consistently under or overstocked then you may need to change your par level.

Branded items

The one commodity you often have to have high stocks of is branded items that have to be specially ordered. All soaps, pens and printed items with logos often need to be ordered in large quantities because it's uneconomical to print them in small batches. So, your stocks may decline to a minimum but after a delivery you may have several months' supply to store somewhere.

One thing to remember is that there can be a long 'lead time' on these (several weeks between order and delivery) so you need to place an order long enough ahead so you don't run out.

In summary: opposing constraints of stock control:

F&B manager	**Controller**
Adequate stocks to avoid:	Minimum investment to avoid:
Refusal of menu items	Excessive capital locked up
Loss of continuity	Pilferage
Reduction of customers (& profit)	Spoilage
Loss of goodwill	Admin/space costs

Stock ratios

There are two ratios that you can use to calculate your stock levels. 'Stock days' are the number of days, on average, that it takes to use up the stock and is by far the most common in use. The other is 'stock turnover' which is how many times the stock is used (turned over) in a period.

$$\text{Stock days} \quad = \quad \frac{\text{Closing stock £}}{\text{Cost £p per day}} \quad \text{days}$$

The cost per day is calculated by taking the usage value (such as food cost of sales) and dividing it by the number of days in the period.

Here's an example:

Beverage stock £6,200, cost of sales for 28 days £3,400

$$\text{Cost per day} \quad = \quad \frac{\text{Cost of sales £}}{\text{Number of days}} \quad = \quad \frac{£3,400}{28} \quad = £121.43$$

$$\text{Stock days} \quad = \quad \frac{\text{Beverage stock £}}{\text{Cost £p per day}} \quad = \quad \frac{£6,200}{£121.43} \quad = 51 \text{ days}$$

Fifty-one days is very long unless you have a large wine list – and a lot of money to have tied up in stock. Could it be reduced?

To work out the stock turnover:

$$\text{Stock turnover} \quad = \quad \frac{\text{Cost of sales £ for the period}}{\text{Closing stock £}} \quad \text{(number of times)}$$

For the above example it would be:

$$\frac{£3,400}{£6,200} \quad = 0.55 \text{ times per 28-day period}$$

Activity

Look at stock levels in your area. Are you over-stocked, under-stocked or just about right – based on the level of usage? Are the items stored adequately according to the regulations? Are there any items of old stock that really should be disposed of?

Cash and stocks

Issuing of stock

Here again the amount of controls you have depends on the type and scale of the operation. If you have a small business and you are monitoring everything yourself then there's no need to record movements of stock – you know what's where.

In a bigger operation, however, there's much more potential for problems and also the management is more likely to want to be able to allocate accurate costs to every department – and as we saw in Chapter 4, cost control is very important to profits. Here you may need to set up a 'requisition system' which means an in-house order book. This may be a paper-based system with duplicate, numbered sheets – the top copy for ordering from the store and the second copy stays in the book (or may be passed to the control office for checking). If you have a stock management system that is accessible in different departments then the transfers can be recorded electronically.

The goods are then transferred from store to outlet. Financial Control will cost these out and charge the department for them. So, if £30 of paper napkins are issued to the cafe and £10 to the kiosk, the value of the stock changes:

In stores reduces by £40	In the cafe increases by £30
	In the kiosk increases by £10

(It's a bit more double-entry book-keeping for you!)

The same can happen if goods are transferred from one unit to another:

The kitchen issues £50 worth (at cost price) of sandwiches, so their stock value is reduced	The bar takes £50 worth of sandwiches to sell to customers, so their stock value is increased

Stocktaking or inventory

We normally think of inventory in terms of food and beverage because those are the most common (although the term 'inventory' is now also used in hotels as the number of rooms available for sale). Food and beverage are often checked every month although many businesses are beginning to question whether this necessary if their other control systems (including par levels) are stringent enough.

Daily spot-checks of key items can indicate problems just as effectively especially if computer systems are installed.

You can also count other items of inventory such as china, glass and silver, linen, cleaning materials, stationery and even maintenance items.

(Ever tried to count light bulbs? Is this *really* a good use of your time?)

It depends on how you account for these – do you consider them 'used' when they are delivered (and so the cost is charged to the P&L) or do you keep stock of them. In any event it's often worth counting high-value items such as silver and crockery just to make sure that items aren't getting broken or lost too much.

There are two ways to count the stock – and you need to do both!

Physical count

This means actually counting every item, weighing every piece of meat and fish and assessing the quantity in every opened bottle of spirit.

If you have a bar-code reader you can just scan most items and then download the data to computer, which will then calculate the stock and its value. Many smaller places may not have this as it's expensive to install and so need to do a physical count, writing the number of items on a list. There's an example of a spreadsheet you can use for inventory in Chapter 9 and as long as you keep the prices up to date then you will (fairly) easily be able to arrive at an accurate cost.

Theoretical count

You need to take the stock of each item – the actual physical count from the previous inventory – and add on the number delivered. You subtract any items that have been lost or damaged or wasted (including beer lost in cleaning the pipes) and then subtract the amount issued to arrive at a 'theoretical stock'. This can then be compared to the physical stock – which *should* be the same.

Here's an example for bottles of a wine:

Opening stock	11
Purchases	35
Total stock available	46
Less issued to restaurant	(32)
Less broken in cellar	(1)
Theoretical stock	13

(It's a similar calculation to cost of sales, which we did in Chapter 2 – only here you are using items rather than value)

Who should take stock?

There are different opinions as to who should actually do the inventory. Some people argue that you need an independent valuer – so an external stocktaker is hired to visit. They will count the stock, give you a valuation and also indicate which items they think are causing you problems. This service obviously costs money.

The other method is to use in-house staff who should be trained in how to count. The usual approach is to have two people do the count – one from financial control and one from the department being counted who both get to know what all the stock is and where it is kept. This method is cheaper but does mean that you have to process all the figures yourselves (although a bar-code scanner can reduce the workload). There is also potential for collusion, the process can take a lot of time, and it needs to be performed when the establishment is closed – so there may be other cost implications.

Valuation and usage calculation

The stock is normally valued at the price at which it is bought – though again there are different views on this. If you buy something that is very volatile in price then one delivery may cost you far more than another – and how do you keep track of which price you paid for which individual item? Hence some businesses always value at the latest price purchased.

We've already looked at calculating cost of sales and this closing stock valuation would form part of that. There's one more calculation to do, though, which is to find the potential sales from the stock you've used.

This means taking the number of items used and valuing them at their selling price. You then compare that to the actual sales you have made. This only works where you have an accurate menu-mix from EPOS or other ways of recording exactly what you sell.

Here's an example:

Number of portions of food used	500
Cost price	£1.50
Selling price	£5.00
Total potential sales	£2,500
Total actual sales	£2,400
Variance (loss)	£100

You need to trace where this £100 of sales (which at £5 each is 20 portions) has gone – then you realise that you transferred them to staff meals one day and forgot to do a requisition for them.

If you hadn't looked at the potential you may have not remembered – which would have meant that CoS was overstated, and staff meals undercharged.

This concludes a review of all the stock control processes that were shown in Figure 7.2. It's an enormous area – whole books have been written on it – and here you have just had an overview of different approaches. Different sectors use different methods of control, depending on their needs and also the availability of stocks – 'just in time' ordering can have a major effect on stock levels and purchasing and hence the controls needed, for instance.

Summary

In this chapter we have looked at the major aspects of controlling cash and stocks. Cash is the 'lifeblood' of the operation – businesses would fail without it – and the opportunities for loss at all stages of the control cycle are huge. Similarly with stocks – if you don't manage them effectively then high values can easily be lost. We have now looked at all the stages of cost control except usage and recipe control, which will be covered in the next chapter on standard costing. You have, therefore:

- Looked at all the key elements in the cycle of working capital
- Reviewed the ways cash can be managed both coming in and going out of the business
- Reviewed all the key stages of movement of stock
- Identified differences of attitude between operations and control.

Cash and stocks

8 Planning and monitoring usage

- Features of raw materials
- Recipe costing
- Standard costing
- Standard costing for payroll
- sales variances

Introduction

This chapter aims to show how costs can be planned and their usage controlled through 'standard costing'. In Chapter 4 we looked at the monitoring of costs and in Chapter 5 at pricing. Here we will consider how to plan spending the correct amount on raw materials. This can be fairly complex in terms of recipes, and a loss of standards can easily cause significant cost variances.

We will then look at identifying deviations from these standards – what is due to variances in price, and what is due to variances in quantity used. We will also consider the specific problems of food and beverage materials, which can cause them to be so difficult to manage.

Standard costing techniques can also be used in other areas. We discussed the management of labour cost earlier, but you can also use the technique to monitor labour cost where a flexible workforce is employed and where productivity is important to the profitability of the business. A further use for the technique is in identifying variations in revenue and considering whether these differences are due to volume or price (or both).

By the end of this chapter you will, therefore, be able to:

- Identify the features of food and beverage raw materials that affect their controllability
- Discuss briefly the process for costing recipes
- Calculate variances according to volume and price
- Use the procedure for labour and other cost variances
- Identify differences in revenues, also due to volume and price.

Features of raw materials

We will first discuss the features of food and beverage that affect the way they are used. Although concentrating on food, many of these are also relevant for beverage.

Perishability

Food is very perishable, particularly if you use a lot of fresh produce (frozen and tinned obviously last longer). Once cooked, health and safety requirements mean that it can be fit for consumption for only one day, and it can be difficult to recycle afterwards. Menus are often designed so that food is prepared to order that can minimise this problem, but other types of facility rely on buffet-style service. Here are some examples:

☐ Carvery (popular in hotels but increasing in staff feeding facilities) which offers very quick service, low staffing costs but potential for high food cost due to lots of waste

☐ Breakfast bar in hotels – few now offer a fully-served breakfast. Guests help themselves to cereals, fruit, juices and bread items, so you need a good display to cater for all needs. These can deteriorate easily if not refrigerated so waste can be high here too (ever tasted 'fizzy' fruit salad that's gone off?)

☐ Lots of facilities have a salad bar, and salad items can be a major cause of food poisoning if they are not replaced frequently – and mayonnaise looks horrid when it's dried on top.

Beverage is less perishable, except for cask beer which can deteriorate rapidly if not cared for.

Desirability

The main concern is that beverage in particular is very desirable for thieves. Spirits can be easily carried out in a handbag or a large internal pocket in a jacket so physical searches of staff may often be required. A policy of staff always showing their bags and pockets whenever they leave can be helpful here. Again it's a question of attitude and management approach.

Mini-case

A trusted employee with nine years' service was caught walking out with a bottle of vodka in her handbag during a routine spot-check. She lost her job and pleaded guilty when prosecuted for theft.

Processes

Food in particular has to go through a range of processes before it is ready for service – ordering, receiving, storage, issue, storage again, manufacture and then service – all of which have potential control problems. This is called the 'control cycle' and we looked at most of the stages in depth in Chapter 7. In this chapter we are just going to concentrate on the final product – the meal or the drink – and how you can ensure that these process controls are correctly used.

Range of products

Another problem is the number of products actually on sale. Very extensive, diverse menus can be very attractive to customers (think of Chinese or Indian food takeaways) but can be difficult control-wise if not carefully planned. If you don't want to cause a lot of waste then you need to ensure that there are lots of base ingredients, such as rice, which can be used in a variety of dishes. The main concern (again) is food poisoning when you have a lot of half-cooked dishes and so, in order to avoid waste (and keep your customers), the menu needs careful planning.

The same is true of beverage – a large wine list looks very attractive but does it sell? It takes a lot of space in your cellar, costs money and eventually may deteriorate. Similarly lots of liqueurs may seem to be a good selling point but if they are rarely ordered then why bother?

Portion and usage control

Beverage

You have by law to sell most items in standard measured quantities so optics, lined glasses or measuring cups should be used. The only exception are cocktails that, although they have a recipe, have fairly variable quantities. A good cocktail maker can achieve good GPs as well as having happy customers.

For standard items, one way of looking at costs is to see what the 'potential' is – say from a bottle of whisky. You calculate how much you've used then see if the sales that were recorded match to this. This is also applicable for beer where you need to be careful not to pour too much into an oversized glass, if you don't have a measured pump. And no, you can't recycle the beer where it's overflowed the glass (but you could keep it aside to see just how much is being wasted, and then pour it down the drain).

Bottles can be stamped when they leave the stores to show that they have been properly issued. This also helps prevent bar staff bringing their own bottles in for sale (and then pocketing the cash). If you are really suspicious then you can mark the bottles (or keep track of the bar code) each day and check what's happening.

Mini-case

A popular bar had recently seen its consumption of gin rise but without any real rise in revenue. Initial suspicions were aimed at the bar staff but as several worked together it would be difficult for one to 'fiddle' without the others knowing. There was a lot of distrust, which made everybody feel very unsettled.

Eventually the manager marked the bottles with invisible pen and monitored them daily. She soon realised that it wasn't the bar staff who were the problem but the cleaner who came in early each morning when nobody else was around and filled up her hip flask. She also admitted to nibbling at the peanuts but nobody had noticed that.

Food

Portion control is crucial to good cost percentages where high volumes are involved. Takeaways often use scoops that measure out the chips, and you will always receive a standard 'squirt' of mayonnaise or ketchup (or both) on your burger. Too much and the customer may have food on their clothes (and it also costs you money) – too little and they will complain of stinginess.

Maintaining food cost through accurate recipe costing and usage is discussed shortly.

Mini-case

A coffee machine in a self-service airport restaurant served 2,000 cups of coffee a day. It was programmed to issue a certain volume of coffee into a cup when the button was pressed. The problem was that there was then no room for customers to add fresh milk (cream pots were okay as they have little volume) and the coffee then split on the saucer, and inevitably on the tray as well (which they then had to run through the dishwasher to remove the stains). This increased the consumption of coffee as well as of paper napkins that were used to clean up the mess.

The controller suggested reducing the measure of coffee by 10%. Result:

- Room for the fresh milk

- Less spillage, meaning happier customers (and so less complaints for the managers to deal with)

- A saving of 10% on coffee, and a substantial amount on paper napkins. There were also savings on water and fuel for the coffee machine and the dishwasher although these couldn't be calculated.

Even for smaller operations it's important to have a standard product for both cost and customer reasons – if you bought an ice cream from a machine and saw that the person in front of you had a larger portion than you, then you'd be annoyed (and if it was your five-year-old child there'd be even more of an upset!).

You can also limit the availability of some items to stop people buying or using them. The traditional conference method is to put a token two chocolate biscuits on the communal plate – and the rest are plain (chocolate ones being more expensive). Another approach is to limit the number of sugar sachets – the more you have available the more will be used (or put in people's pockets). Fast food and in-store restaurants often don't put out sachets of ketchup and mayonnaise – the customer has to ask for them – because customers may take them home for their own use.

Activity   Be a customer somewhere such as a pub or cafe – and sit where you can observe the staff (at the bar is best). Watch what they do, in serving the customers and in controlling costs. Are they really efficient or just appear to be? Are they operating in the best interests of the business, or only themselves? See if you can spot wastage. Are the cash controls adequate? Then when you go back to your facility you can see if you are able to use anything that you've learned.

Recipe costing

Accurate costing of recipes is crucial to the entire process of food control (and beverage to a lesser extent). If you don't have standards established then there's a danger that chefs will use whatever they wish, both in terms of amount and product specification – so you may have prime steak used for a lasagne, for instance. Standard recipes are important because:

☐ A standard process is used which produces a standard quality product

☐ Training and activity rotation become easier

☐ Each customer receives a product of the same size and quality

☐ Costs remain stable

☐ Chefs know what they are doing.

This doesn't necessarily take away their creativity but just ensures they stick to basic instructions.

How the costing is done

1. The recipe is carefully worked out and a standard batch size (which could be one or 100s) is established. This means every single ingredient, including pinches of salt and half-teaspoons of spices.

2. The cost of each ingredient is calculated.

3. The costs of all ingredients for the batch are added to give a batch cost.

4. The cost per portion is calculated, and maybe the cost or GP percentage.

Many businesses now use software packages to calculate recipe costs, usually integrated into their purchasing and stock management systems. These take the purchase price (from the purchasing section of the system), the yield of a commodity (such as six slices per tomato) and then convert this into a cost per dish. Costs can be easily amended to reflect current market prices and so update the GP. If you don't have this type of system

– which can be expensive for a small business to operate and so may not be cost-effective – then you can use a spreadsheet system to help you calculate your recipe costs.

Standard recipes are essential in many sectors. They show the catering assistant just what has to be used for a specific dish or meal and the manager knows exactly what this will cost. For sectors such as airline catering or any large-volume business this can mean a massive difference in costs.

Mini-case

A sandwich production unit presented sandwiches on plates rather than in packets – this was an upmarket operation although with very high volumes – up to 5,000 a day. The garnish on the sandwich was a lettuce leaf, a slice of cucumber and a slice of tomato. A new supervisor with little knowledge of costs decided that one slice of tomato didn't look generous enough so ordered the assistants to add one more. The cost for that single day was £158 (5,000 slices of tomato, at 6 slices per tomato = 833 tomatoes at £0.19 each). It also played havoc with the ordering processes – they had to stop adding the extra slice when they saw they were going to run out of tomatoes.

Here's an example of a recipe:

Tomato and mint sorbet

Ingredients (for 10 portions)	Recipe amount	Cost price (£)
Plum tomatoes	2 kg	2.00
Mint leaves	3 bunches	2.20
Icing sugar	425 gm	0.45
Lemon juice	1 tbsp	0.15
	Total	4.80
	Cost per portion	0.48
	Selling price at 65% gross profit	1.37

Standard costing

Standard costing is a term normally used for finding out the budget – 'standard' – cost of a recipe according to the exact recipe specification. Once you have standard recipe costs established then you can compare them to what actually occurs and see where differences appear. You can show whether any change in cost for producing an item is due to differences in the use of ingredients or in the price of them.

For some sectors this may not be important but in sectors with very tight margins and high volumes, such as in-flight catering, any slight variances may mean the difference between profit and loss on a contract. Once you know about the technique you can use it to manipulate your estimates – and perhaps see the financial effect of different specifications. It can also be used for analysing variances in labour and sales and we'll look at these later in the chapter.

Understanding, and calculating, the technique can seem quite complicated so we will work through this step by step.

How to do it

Let's look at the production of a menu item – say scrambled eggs. For 10 portions of scrambled eggs you need 20 eggs (we'll ignore the butter for cooking) which cost £0.20 each, total £4.00.

If you showed the cost of these in a diagram it would look like Figure 8.1.

Figure 8.1: Basic cost

Price	NORMAL				
£4.00					
£3.00		20 eggs @ £0.20 = £4.00			
£2.00					
£0.00					
Volume	5	10	15	20	eggs

But if we were to use five extra eggs as ingredients for the same number of portions (we were generous) then this would cost more, see Figure 8.2.

This extra cost would mean that the scrambled eggs would cost £5.00 instead of £4.00 for the same 10 portions without any extra sales.

Figure 8.2: Basic cost plus extra usage

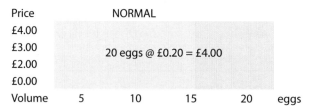

Price		NORMAL			EXTRA USAGE	
£4.00						
£3.00		20 eggs @ £0.20 = £4.00			5 @ £0.20 = £1.00	Total
£2.00						cost
£0.00						£5.00
Volume	5	10	15	20	25	

A further problem could be that an egg shortage caused a price rise or that the chef decided to use organic rather than free range, as well as using the extra eggs. The extra 5 pence per egg (now 25p instead of 20p) obviously affects all those 25 eggs that you are now using, see Figure 8.3.

Figure 8.3: Basic cost plus extra usage and extra price

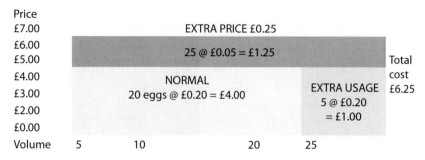

This means that although you originally costed or budgeted for £4.00 (the 'standard cost') the actual cost was £6.25.

Methods of standard costing

There are two methods of calculating standard cost variances, both of which produce the same result. Different people use different methods, so choose the one that suits you best. The convention is that we look at usage first and price second.

Here's the first way of doing it. Books tend to be a bit theoretical when showing this which can be off- putting but if you go through step-by-step then it's not too tedious.

Method 1

This finds the difference first and then calculates its cost.

1. Find the budgeted (standard) usage of each ingredient from the standard recipe
2. Calculate the cost of each ingredient
3. Calculate the cost of the ingredients that were actually used

Now you can find the variances.

4. Find the usage variance by taking the *difference* in ingredients times the *standard* (budgeted, or original) price
5. Find the price variance by taking the *difference* in price of the ingredients times the Actual quantity (the amount used)

It's easier if you see an example (using those scrambled eggs again):

	Ingredients	Price (£)	Cost (£)	
Budget (recipe says)	20 eggs	@ 0.20	4.00	*should have cost*
Actual	25 eggs	@ 0.25	6.25	*actually did cost*
Variance		0.05	2.25	ADVERSE – *spent too much*

The difference is expressed as favourable (good) or adverse (bad) or FAV and ADV for short.

These are Steps 1 to 3 as above. So you know the total variance is £2.25 (adverse), but how much of this is due to volume (quantity of eggs here) and how much to extra price?

	Ingredients	Price (£)	Cost (£)	
Step 4 – Usage variance	5 eggs	@ 0.20	1.00	ADV
Step 5 – Price variance	25 eggs	@ 0.05	1.25	ADV
Total			2.25	ADV

Look at the three diagrams (Figures 8.1–3) if it helps – Steps 1 and 2 are the Budget, Step 4 adds the extra usage, Step 5 adds the extra price, which all adds up to the Actual result (Step 3).

Method 2

This calculates the value first and then finds the variance:

1. Take the standard quantity (recipe ingredients) and multiply it by the standard (budget) price

   In textbooks this is standard quantity × standard price or STD Q × STD P

2. Change the quantity to what you actually used:

   Actual quantity × standard price (ACT Q × STD P)

3. Find the difference between the two – this is the usage variance

4. Change the price to what you actually paid:

   Actual quantity × actual price (ACT Q × ACT P)

5. Find the difference between the two – this is the price variance.

   So, using the above example:

		(£)	
STD Q × STD P	20 eggs × £0.20	4.00	
ACT Q × STD P	25 eggs × £0.20	5.00	
Usage variance		£1.00	ADV
ACT Q × ACT P	25 eggs × £0.25	6.25	
Price variance		£1.25	ADV
Total variance		£2.25	ADV

Let's try another example – simplified to just one ingredient although in practice most recipes have several ingredients all of which can vary in usage and price.

	Cost (£)	Usage	Total (£)	
Standard food cost	4.80	140	672.00	
Actual food cost	4.70	130	611.00	
Difference	0.10	10	61.00	FAV

Standard quantity × budget price	140 × £4.80 =	672.00	
Actual quantity × budget price	130 × £4.80 =	624.00	
Usage variance		48.00	FAV
Actual quantity × actual price	130 × £4.70 =	611.00	
Price variance		13.00	FAV
Total variance		61.00	FAV

Exercise 8.1

Now it's your turn! Here's the standard food cost of two ingredients:

Ingredient F – 0.25 kg per portion at £2.00 per kg, a total of 255 kg is used, total cost £510.00

Ingredient O – 0.125 kg per portion at £2.40 per kg, a total of 127.5 kg is used, total cost £306.00

So the total budgeted standard cost is £816.00. The actual food cost for the ingredients is:

Actual food cost	kg	£/kg	Per portion (£)	usage kg	Total (£)
Ingredient F	0.26	1.90	0.494	265.2	503.88
Ingredient O	0.175	2.60	0.455	178.5	464.10
Total			0.949		967.98

Where has the extra £151.98 cost (the difference between £816.00 and £967.98) occurred?

You'll find a worked answer at the end of the book.

Tip

The recipe has two ingredients, so you will need to work them out separately. You can then add the total variances together to find out the overall difference.

The technique works for price falls as well as rises. What about using too little, or if prices are lower – is this a problem? Well, accounting-wise it may not be (you've cut costs) but this is a quality issue. You need to maintain your quality standards so your customers know what to expect. Cutting costs can harm the business long-term – what you want is to be more efficient in what you use, rather than wasting resources.

Activity

Look at a food item that you are involved in (or can see in a restaurant). Can you calculate how much extra cost there would be if you used too much?

Monitoring usage

Standard costing for payroll

We've concentrated on F&B, which is the most common area where standard costing is used but we can also use the technique for other areas.

As we've seen, payroll is traditionally fairly fixed but businesses are now trying to be more flexible in their scheduling, hopefully without upsetting staff.

First let's use the standard costing way of finding differences in the cost of overall payroll.

Exercise 8.2

Here's a budget (standard) and actual staff cost for two jobs:

Budget staff cost	Rate (£)	Hours	Total (£)
Catering assistants	7.00	120	840
General assistants	6.50	160	1,040
Total			1,880

Actual staff cost	Rate (£)	Hours	Total (£)
Catering assistants	7.10	110	781
General assistants	6.40	170	1,088
Total			1,869
Total variance			11 FAV

Can you work out for each category how much of the difference is related to pay rate and how much to the number of hours worked?

You could also use it to plan ahead. If you have a current situation of staff working certain hours at a set rate and a proposal is made to change these, then the same type of exercise can be performed.

Here's a scenario you could use. The housekeeping manager employs cleaners for 300 student rooms. Each cleaner is expected to clean 25 rooms a day at a cost of £2.38 per room per day (including benefits), total standard cost of £59.50 per day.

However, a new agreement is proposed by the staff union which suggests a pay increase of 5% and a reduction of the number of rooms cleaned to 24 per day. How much would each of these options cost? What would be the difference for both changes (reduction of rooms and pay increase), separately and in total?

Sales variances

All the above have been costs – but what about using the technique for sales too? Let's try this with a package price for a short-break holiday. We can see what the effect would be on sales if we decided to offer a £50 discount per holiday.

	Normal budget	Forecast with discount	Variance
Holiday guests	1,350	1,550	150
Package price	£500	£450	(£50)
Sales	£675,000	£697,500	£22,500

Now let's calculate how much of these extra £22,500 sales are due to extra people, and how much was lost due to the discount).

	Rooms	Rate £	Sales £
Guests – budget			
Guests- forecast			
Variance			

Volume (usage)			
Price			
Total			

Remember that it's easier to find the usage variance first, then the price.

Exercise 8.3

Here's another exercise to try – this time for a menu item.

	Covers	Selling price £	Sales £
Budget	3,320	£6.75	
Actual	3,170	£6.80	
Variance			

Volume (usage)			
Price			
Total			

Exercise 8.4

Now try an exercise on accommodation:

	Rooms	Selling price (£)	Sales £
Budget	50	79.50	
Actual	55	77.50	
Variance			

Volume (usage)			
Price			
Total			

Monitoring usage

There's also another technique described in the textbooks called Flexible Budgets. By combining the two techniques, you can compare the GP levels as well.

Activity   Talk to managers in your organisation. Do they use standard costing as a technique? If they don't, could they? Why not try looking at payroll costs or at sales and see if you can analyse variances using this approach?

Summary

In this eighth chapter we have discussed the technique of standard costing which is mainly used for analysing variances for recipes. The differences relating to usage and to price of the ingredients can be separately identified so that the manager can then take action where possible.

Standard costing can also be used for other purposes. It can show where payroll costs have not matched budget, again identifying variances due to volume (number of staff, or hours worked) and price (rates of pay). Additionally it can be used to analyse variances in sales revenue, also showing where shortfalls or overages have occurred in average spends and in customer numbers. These can be used in all sectors of the industry – for leisure and tourism as well as food and beverage and rooms areas.

You have, therefore:

- Discussed the purpose of standard recipes
- Reviewed in diagrammatic format the way that standard costs are identified
- Calculated variances due to volume and price
- Identified other areas where the technique might be used
- Calculated a range of other variances.

9 Using spreadsheets for management tasks

- The basics of spreadsheet design
- Using spreadsheeets for different tasks
- Presenting results
- Practice with spreadsheets

Introduction

In this chapter we are going to see how using spreadsheets can help you with many of the control tasks that we have discussed in the different chapters. We'll also see how you can use graphs and charts (hand-drawn and by spreadsheet) to help in decision-making and presenting results.

We will look at some of the simple techniques that can make spreadsheets easier to use on a frequent basis and at some of the shortcuts you can take. Incorporating some basic design features can help with ongoing usage, and with enabling others to use spreadsheets that you have designed. The use of charts and how they can help with presenting complex information in a simpler way will also be considered.

It's assumed that you have a basic knowledge of spreadsheets. If some of this is boring because you're at a higher level of competence, then please move on. There's a refresher exercise to revise skills and perhaps practise some new ones, and some suggestions about using spreadsheets for personal tasks.

By the end of this chapter, therefore, you should be able to:

- Comprehend the basic principles of spreadsheet design
- Practise a range of techniques to improve speed and efficiency
- Comprehend the variety of areas where spreadsheets can be used
- Draw a chart to scale by hand
- Create a chart using a spreadsheet.

The basics of spreadsheet design

The following basic principles are adapted from Peter Harris's book *Profit Planning* – see the reading list for further details. They are:

☐ Design on paper first

☐ Use separate Input and Output worksheets

☐ And maybe another for 'workings out' (or add this at the end of the Input area)

☐ Test your results.

Designing on paper

The temptation with doing a spreadsheet is just to sit at the computer and do it, without planning. This works for some people, but can waste a lot of time.

If you take a piece of rough paper and write down all the things you need to do for that particular spreadsheet, you'll have a better idea of how much space it's going to take.

Ask yourself the following questions:

☐ What's the purpose of this spreadsheet? Is it very complex?

☐ Who is going to use it – just you or lots of other people? If it's others will they need instructions about how to use it?

☐ Do you trust their skills?

☐ Will the spreadsheet need to be significantly amended at a future date, or just updated?

☐ How many reports need to be generated from one batch of input data?

☐ Do you need several different worksheets within the same file?

☐ Are you going to have to link this spreadsheet file to another?

☐ Is there a requirement for the report/s to fit in a specific space, such as an A4 piece of paper?

☐ Do you need colour and different fonts?

☐ What about charts?

☐ Are you going to have to copy a chart into another file (e.g. Word)?

☐ If you're really skilled, what about (for instance) macros, hyperlinks to other documents, spreadsheets or websites?

And so on...

Once you've done this then you can make a design – still on paper, though. You can roughly sketch out what will go where on the different worksheets. Some older textbooks suggest working out the formulas although there normally isn't a need to do this, unless you are designing something very complex.

Try and make it as easy to use as possible with columnar formats (working in parallel with the same columns as you move down) and using the top left-hand corner of the screen first, then paging down rather than across.

Tip   If you can, work out the results by hand first – then you can check these against the output from the spreadsheet.

Input and Output areas

Using separate Input and Output worksheets, and maybe another for 'workings out', means that:

☐ You keep all your raw data *(input* – your original numbers – those that you key in) separate from

☐ All the *output* which is the results – Output areas are all formulas – no actual figures are keyed in there.

Ideally you have a separate worksheet within the file for the input, and then several for output depending on what type of reports you need. For instance, for a P&L, the input would be the trial balance (all the source data you need) and the output the departmental reports, possibly each on a separate worksheet. The front page would then be a total of all the departmental reports. This means that the source data (trial balance – please read up about this if you need to) only gets entered once and, when updated each month, immediately changes all the reports – much easier than moving around lots of different worksheets.

Here's an example for a very small P&L statement:

Input

This is your source data – it's all raw numbers – on one worksheet (could be actually called 'Input' if you wish, or perhaps 'source data'):

Input worksheet:

(Note: italics are used just to differentiate here between input and output data – they're not at all necessary.)

Cell	A	B
1	*Sales including VAT*	*28800*
2	*Payroll*	*6800*
3	*Expenses*	*2400*
4	*Customers*	*5000*
5	*Capacity*	*6000*
6	*VAT rate*	*0.20*

Workings out

These are any intermediate calculations you need to do (for instance, extract VAT). This could be a separate worksheet or just entered further down the input column. Here you type in the formula to extract the VAT from the sales.

Cell	A	B	Formula in cell B10
10	Sales less VAT	24000	=B1/(1+B6)

(Don't worry about the formula – the '(1+B6)' will be explained later.)

Now you have the net figures that you need, ready to do the P&L.

These are results and are calculated by formulas from the input worksheet – there is no source data in the output worksheet.

Output worksheet

Cell	A	B	Formula in B cells	
1	Sales	£24,000	= Input!B10	(all formatted as £)
2	Payroll	(£6,800)	=-Input!B2	
3	Expenses	(£2,400)	=-Input!B3	
4	Profit	£14,800	=sum(B1:B3)	
5	Average spend per customer	£4.80	=B1/Input!B4	(formatted as £p)
6	Occupancy	83.3%	=Input!B4/Input!B5	(formatted as % to 1 decimal place)
7	Profit per customer	£2.96	=B4/Input!B4	(formatted as £p)
8	Profit percentage	61.7%	=B4/B1	(formatted as % to 1 decimal place)

(Where it says 'Input!' in the B cells above it means that the spreadsheet has gone to the Input worksheet to get the data from the particular cell. So – cell B1 in the output worksheet has looked in cell B10 in the input worksheet to find the number 24000. Where there is a minus sign in the formula it is saying 'go to the cell, find this number and show it as a minus figure'.)

Activity   Choose one of the earlier exercises and plan on paper how it would look on a spreadsheet.

Spreadsheet exercise

Objective: to practise many of the basic spreadsheet skills using Excel in order to create a rooms departmental statement, utilising the basic spreadsheet design principles. You will also create a simple pie chart.

This is what you want to achieve (the first section is *input*, the second *output*):

Input worksheet used for *source data*.

Cell	A	B	
1	Source data		
2			
3	Rooms revenue	£12,000	
4	Payroll	£1,680	
5	Expenses	£940	
6	Rooms sold	150	
7	Rooms available	200	

(The numbers have been formatted for £ and commas to make them easier to use.)

Output worksheet used for *results*

Cell	A	B	C
1	Rooms P&L		
2			
3	Rooms revenue	£12,000	100.0%
4	Payroll	(£1,680)	-14.0%
5	Expenses	(£940)	-7.8%
6	**Rooms profit**	£9,380	78.2%
7	Average room rate	£80.00	
8	Room occupancy	75.0%	

You will see that some items appear twice. This is the design feature we mentioned earlier where we are trying to keep the raw or source data (called 'input' – those shown in *italics* above) separate from the results (called 'output'), which makes it easier to manage the spreadsheet. This is particularly relevant when you have very large reports.

Note: Click – means use the left button of the mouse, ↵ means Enter

1 *Start a new worksheet and name the file.* Start Excel. Click the Office button (top left-hand corner) and then New, Blank Workbook if you need to. To save the file – Office, Save As, and title 'Rooms P&L' as the file name.

2 *Retitle this first worksheet (currently titled Sheet 1)* You will then see, at the bottom of your screen, that the tab is titled 'Sheet 1'. Double-click on this until the title goes black. Type in the new name 'Input' and ↵ . You could also click on the tab, right-click and Rename.

3 *Type the labels as above.* Starting at cell A1, type Input, ↵. Note that the cursor automatically moves to cell A2. Move to cell A3 and type the five labels, as shown on the Input table on the previous page.

4 *Repeat stages 2 & 3 for the Output worksheet.* Click on Sheet 2. Rename this as Output and then type the relevant labels, again as shown above.

5 *Note that the column widths need adjustment.* Put the cursor on the line between the titles of columns A and B (grey shaded) until you see a black cross (you may need to click on the A column first). Hold the mouse down and move it to the right until the column widens enough for your needs. Repeat for other worksheet.

6 *Embolden the words 'Rooms Profit'.* Output worksheet, Cell A6; hold the mouse down to highlight the word 'Profit'. Move the mouse up to the Bold icon (within the Home toolbar) and click.

7 *Underline title – 'Rooms P&L'.* Cell A1, highlight the words and Underline.

8 *Italicise the source (input) data cells.* Input, block A3 to B7 as above, click on Italic icon.

9 *Enter the raw data*. Type in the numbers as shown in Input, B3-B7 ONLY.

10 *Save the file again*. Click on the Save icon (a floppy-disk shape next to the Office icon).

11 *You now need to create the departmental statement – start with the rooms revenue*. Output, go to B3, click and type the = sign. Then click on Input, place cursor on B3 and ↵. You will see that the cell says '12000'. If you look at the formula line (just below the toolbars) you will see that the formula says '=Input!B3' (and NOT 12,000).

12 *Repeat for the payroll in B4*. You can either repeat the above action or just Copy the cell above. But – as this is a cost you really want to subtract this from the revenue, so you need to Edit the formula. Go to the Formula bar. Click on this and move the cursor between the '=' and the word 'Input'. Insert a minus sign and ↵. You will see that cell B4 now says (1680) – or -1680, depending on the set-up of your machine.

13 *Enter expense formula*. You can do this in two ways. Click on the B4 cell and either Copy (icon or right-click with the mouse) and then Paste to B10, or Fill Down to the next cell. You need to make sure if you are Filling Down that a little black cross appears on the bottom right-hand corner of B4 – this indicates the correct function is being used. Note that the formula in B5 is correct and the number (-940) displayed.

14 *Calculate the profit*. Cell B6. Click on the AutoSum icon ∑ (in the Editing section of the Home toolbar) – it will suggest the range of cells to add together. If this is fine then ↵, if not then block the correct range and then ↵. This will add the revenue, and subtract the costs, to give a profit.

15 *Format these as Currency*. Block B3 to B6. Click on the Currency icon (Number section of Home toolbar). You really need these as round pounds (no pence) so click twice on the Decrease decimal icon (also in Number). If the costs are now set up as a minus and you wanted brackets you can change this using Custom formatting. When you become more skilled you may wish to Edit this Custom function to display numbers in the way you prefer.

16 *Calculate the Average Room rate*. Cell B7. You want to use the Revenue (B3) divided by the Rooms sold (Input B6) so in Output cell B7 type '=' , click on B3, type ' /', then click on Input cell B6 ↵ . Format this as Currency to 2 decimal places.

17 *Calculate the Room Occupancy*. Cell B8. Type '=', click on Input B6, type '/', click on Input B7, ↵ Format as a Percentage (using the % icon) to 1 decimal place (note that if you format as % you don't need to use the x100 or /100 as you would if you calculated by hand).

18 *Align the figures to the right of their cells if necessary*. Block B3:B8 and click on the Align Right icon (in the Alignment section).

19 *Save again.* Click on the Save icon.

20 *You now need to calculate the costs and profits as a percentage of sales.* Output Cell C4. Enter formula '=B4/B3', format as % to 1 decimal point. Copy to the next cell down. Look at the result in C5 – it isn't correct and you'll see that it says '=B10/B9'. You need to FIX the cell reference of B8 so that all items calculate as a percentage of this. Go back to C4 and Edit the formula to read '= B4/B$3'. A quick way to do this is to hit the F4 key whilst the cursor is on the correct part of the formula (the B3) – hitting it once, twice or three times will give you different options as to which element of the formula is fixed. Then fill this down to C5 and C6. You will now see that each cell refers to B3 – the $ sign fixes the cell reference. Here we used it to fix the Row, but you can also fix the Column by putting a $ in front of the column letter, or fix both. If you wish you can copy the formula back to C3, the rooms revenue expressed as a % of itself. Also, the % is a minus figure (because that's how the original figure is shown). If you don't want this then put a minus sign after the = within the formula.

21 *Check the alignment of the % (should be Right).* If necessary then correct these.

22 *Change the font for the entire worksheet.* Click on the grey square above the row titles and to the left of the column titles – this will block everything. Click on the font title above and format both font and size to a style you prefer. If you have chosen a larger font then you may see '########' (or an odd-looking number that includes E+10) appearing in the cell, rather than the number you expected. This is because the column is not wide enough for the number to be displayed. To correct this, simply either widen the cell, change the font, or (if feasible) reduce the number of decimal points.

Congratulations – you have now created a simple profit statement!

Creating a chart

Now, suppose you wanted to put this information into a chart format. The best way to display this information would be a Pie Chart.

1 *Select the data in the Output sheet.* Highlight A4 to B6.

2 *Use Chart Wizard.* Click on the Insert toolbar (top line, next to Home on the left), then choose Pie within the Charts section.

3 *Choose your chart type.* Click on Pie, then choose the type of pie chart. You'll see a chart appear on your spreadsheet. If you want to change the colours then there are options shown at the top of the screen. Then click on the Chart Layout (within the Design toolbar) and choose Layout 1.

4   *Title your chart*. Click on Chart Title within the chart itself, and type Rooms P&L. The text will appear in the formula line towards the top of the screen. When you hit ↵ the title will change.

5   *Underline and embolden the title*. Click on the title Rooms P&L on the chart (but not on the whole chart) – you'll see that it appears in a text box. Format this by right-clicking then using the **B** and <u>U</u> icons on the pop-up menu.

6   *Save your file*

Using spreadsheets for different tasks

Now we need to look at using spreadsheets for different jobs. Here are some exercises that you can try yourself if you have access to a spreadsheet.

Calculating ratios

We have already done some above. Why not take the Food and Beverage exercise from Chapter 4 and see if you can set it up on a spreadsheet? The information from the question goes into the Input area, and then the Output is the report and the ratios. You may not need a 'workings out' section here.

Pricing

You can use spreadsheets for pricing in different ways – depending on what type of pricing method you use. Later on, when we look at charts, we will practise setting up a break-even chart. Here are a couple of examples of how you can calculate prices using the GP method and the Contribution method.

First, GP – suppose you had costs of £4.00 and wanted to see the price that would emerge at different levels of GP%.

Source data (Input)

Cell	A	B	C	D
1	Costs	£4.00		
2		Scenario 1	Scenario 2	Scenario 3
3	Gross profit required	30%	40%	50%
4	Cost percentage	70%	60%	50%
5				
6	VAT rate	20%		

Now here's the formulas for the Output area which calculates the selling price, and the menu price including VAT.

Cell	A	B	C	D
1		Scenario A	Scenario B	Scenario C
2	Costs	='Input'!$B$1	='Input'!$B$1	='Input'!$B$1
3	Cost level	='Input'!B4	='Input'!C4	='Input'!D4
4	Selling price	=B2/B3	=C2/C3	=D2/D3
5	Menu price including VAT	=B4*(1+'Input'!$B$6)	=C4*(1+'Input'!$B$6)	=D4*(1+'Input'!$B$6)

Note that the 'grossing up' technique is used (taking the cost and dividing it by the cost % to achieve the SP). So the answer will show as:

Cell	A	B	C	D
1		Scenario A	Scenario B	Scenario C
2	Costs	£4.00	£4.00	£4.00
3	Cost level	70%	60%	50%
4	Selling price	£5.71	£6.67	£8.00
5	Menu price including VAT	£6.85	£8.00	£ 9.60

A couple of extra tips for you.

Use of the $ sign

This 'fixes' the cell reference. You notice that every SP calculation needs the basic cost figure (£4.00) which is in cell B2. If you set up the correct formula in cell B12 *and* include the $ sign as shown then you can copy (or Fill Right) the cell across. The B column stays fixed but the second half of the formula changes to the C and D columns. The action is repeated to add the VAT. The quick way to do this is using the F4 key.

☐ A single press of the F4 key – puts the $ in front of both – fixes both

☐ A second press of F4 – puts the $ in front of the row- fixes the row reference

☐ A third press of F4 – puts the $ in front of the column – fixes the column reference

This saves a lot of time when building complex sheets. You just need to double-check the formula in the new cells.

Calculating VAT (or adding any percentage figure on to a base)

You'll see that the formula reads * (times) and then in brackets (1+) and the cell reference (such as 1+C14). This says take the original amount and multiply it by itself and the percentage amount of the cell (here 20%). It's the same as using a calculator where you multiply by 1.20 to add VAT. If you wanted to add 17.5% to the total the formula would be * (1+ 17.5%).

Next – an example for the contribution method. Suppose you have variable costs of £25 and want to see what contribution percentage can be achieved at different sales levels – say £70, £75 and £80 (we'll ignore VAT this time, but you could extract it by dividing by 1+ 20%).

Here's the source data:

Cell	A	B	C	D
1	Variable costs	£25.00		
2		Scenario A	Scenario B	Scenario C
3	Selling price	£70.00	£75.00	£80.00

The answer is:

	Scenario A	Scenario B	Scenario C
Selling price	£70.00	£75.00	£80.00
Variable costs	-£25.00	-£25.00	-£25.00
Contribution	£45.00	£50.00	£55.00
CM%	64.3%	66.7%	68.8%

The formulas are:

Cell	A	B	C	D
1		Scenario A	Scenario B	Scenario C
2	Selling price	='Input'!B3	='Input'!C3	='Input'!D3
3	Variable costs	=-'Input'!$B$1	=-'Input'!$B$1	=-'Input'!$B$1
4	Contribution	=SUM(B2:B3)	=SUM(C2:C3)	=SUM(D2:D3)
5				
6	CM%	=B4/B2	=C4/C2	=D4/D2

You'll see that the variable cost formula has a minus sign in front of the $B which then means that it is subtracted (and shows in red on screen). The percentage takes the CM as a % of sales and is formatted as a percentage to 1 decimal place (the % icon).

These are rather simple as examples and for one calculation a calculator may be quicker – but if you have lots to do then it's worth setting up. Once you have the formulas established for one item then you can copy for other items – providing that the $ signs are set correctly.

Stocktaking

Lots of you may already have stock control packages, often including bar-code scanners to scan items which then automatically download to computer. This will update the stock list, calculate inventories and then give a total stock value. Other businesses may choose to use a spreadsheet to calculate stock values, but you do need to take care.

This may be one situation in which you don't use a separate input worksheet, given the number of additions you may need to make each time for new items. If your inventory is stable (that is, you don't add new items, or new sizes) then you may be able to use one area for input and another for output.

Columns

Commodity	Unit size	Price	Quantity	Value

It's suggested that you write-protect and/or colour those columns you don't need to use often, depending on how reliable your inputting is (or somebody else's).

You could use a separate worksheet for each area (kitchen, stores, restaurants, etc.) and then another to total them all. You may also want to separate the commodities in which case your summary sheet might look like Table 9.1.

Table 9.1: Sample summary sheet

	Stores	Kitchen	Restaurant	Bar food	TOTAL COMMODITY
Meat & fish					
Dairy					
Bakery					
Tinned goods					
Frozen foods					
Herbs & spices					
Prepared foods					
Snacks					
Miscellaneous					
Drink for cooking					
TOTAL STOCK					

Each cell should contain a formula that takes the relevant total from the relevant stock sheet, so that if you amend your sheets or stock then the figures will stay accurate. The total columns then SUM the rows or columns.

To calculate the overall cost of sales you need the standard formula, given in Chapter 2 when we discussed the P&L report.

If you have an EPOS system then the sales report may also give you a theoretical cost of sales figure, based on your menus and pricing system.

You can also use a spreadsheet to calculate the items used and then their value. This is really useful for high-value items such as wine. For instance:

Commodity	Opening stock	Plus purchases	Less transfers	Less closing stock	Cost	Value of stock used
Whisky						
Gin						

The value of the stock used can then be compared to the sales achieved, by different commodity, so you can see whether there are losses.

Forecasting

Spreadsheets can be really helpful for saving time in projecting sales and profits, say for a week, based on changing volumes and sales.

For instance (you could fill in some source data yourself):

	Monday	Tuesday	Wednesday	Thursday	Friday	Saturday	Sunday
Visitors							
Spend							
Variable cost							
Fixed cost							

Note that fixed costs *per day* and the variable costs *per visitor* remain unchanged, so that you can treat all this as input data. Only the number of visitors would change, so the output would look like this:

	Monday	Tuesday	Wednesday	Thursday	Friday	Saturday	Sunday	Total
Visitors								
Sales								
Variable cost								
Contribution								
Fixed cost								
Profit								
Break-even point								

You can then see that some days make more profit, others less, and can plan accordingly.

Activity

If you have access to a spreadsheet then try setting this one up, practising all we've talked about so far. If you haven't got access, then you could just use a calculator.

Spreadsheets

Market segmentation

If you're in a rooms department in a hotel you may have lots of market segments all of which vary by day and by week. For this you can set up really complex formulas to analyse revenue and occupancy by day, and then show the patterns over a period.

For instance, another activity:

Rooms sold (fill some numbers in yourself if you wish)

	Monday	Tuesday	Wednesday	Thursday	Friday	Saturday	Sunday
Rooms available	100	100	100	100	100	100	100
Rack rate							
Leisure							
Corporate							

Room occupancy (calculate the percentages)

	Monday	Tuesday	Wednesday	Thursday	Friday	Saturday	Sunday
Rooms available	100	100	100	100	100	100	100
Rack rate							
Leisure							
Corporate							

By manipulating the percentages you can see how much revenue you can generate so please add some average room rates and then calculate the revenues.

Room rate and revenue

	Monday	Tuesday	Wednesday	Thursday	Friday	Saturday	Sunday
Avg. room rate							
Rack rate							
Leisure							
Corporate							
Revenue							
Rack rate							
Leisure							
Corporate							

Presenting results

Now let's look at charts and how you can use them for forecasting and reporting figures.

Some charts are best drawn by hand but a spreadsheet chart is good for display, especially if you can use colour. You can choose the colours on screen and for printing, but if you do not have a colour printer the different categories will print in shades of grey.

A chart done by a spreadsheet is a *picture* – it gives you an instant appreciation of what you are trying to say, far more easily than words. Charts can be very useful for presenting results in a meeting, where it's the overall impression you're trying to give – not an exact result.

Charts can be copy-pasted from a spreadsheet into a document or PowerPoint presentation, and then re-sized to fit your needs.

There are three main types that are likely to be of benefit to you – pie charts, column/bar charts and line charts.

Pie charts

These are useful for splitting something into component parts – like slices of a pie or pizza. So, we can use it for splitting total customers into market segments or total sales into different types. We can also split the 'sales pie' into different costs and profit. We practised one earlier as part of the spreadsheet exercise. Figure 9.1 shows an example.

Figure 9.1: Pie chart

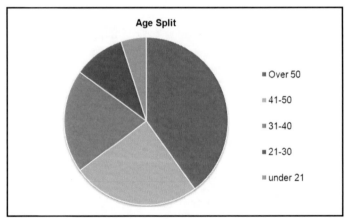

Column/bar charts

Column or Bar charts can show comparative numbers, day-by-day or week-by-week, for example. You can show two sets of numbers side by side as well. Depending on the type of data you can show them either vertically (Column) or horizontally (Bar). They are good for showing changes in staffing levels or for forecasting. Figure 9.2 is an example.

Line charts

This can be either a single zigzag line to show, for instance, sales levels or several lines to show different items. A break-even chart is a line chart, which we'll look at shortly. Figure 9.3 shows the same sales figures from the column chart but in a line chart format.

Figure 9.2: Column chart

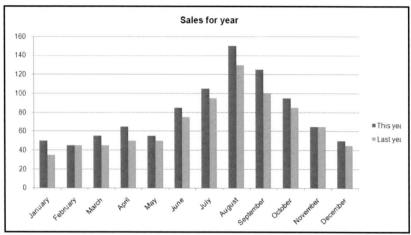

Figure 9.3: Line chart

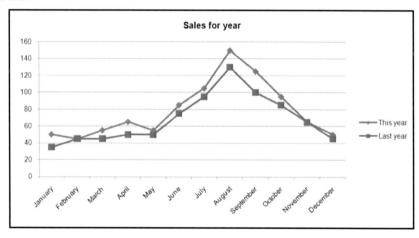

Charts for decision making

Here you want to be accurate – a chart is a tool here rather than just a picture. It's worth taking time over so that it really will 'add value' to your decisions. For instance, if you were trying to find out the BEP you would want it to show exactly where the sales exceed the total costs. It's also useful to be able to look at different scenarios – for instance to plot different sales lines for different selling prices, all with the same costs. This will then give you three alternative BEPs.

Figure 9.4 shows what a break-even chart looks like.

☐ The Y-axis (vertical – the letter stands up!) is the sales and costs in money.

☐ The X-axis (horizontal) is the volume in units. The units could be customers or numbers of items, like cups of coffee.

Figure 9.4: Break-even chart

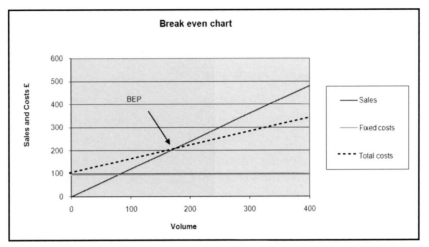

☐ The main diagonal line from the zero point is sales.

☐ The horizontal line parallel to the X-axis is the fixed costs (FC) – you have the same cost if your volume of sales is zero or high volume. The variable costs then get added on *top* of this fixed cost line because you need to find the total costs if you want the BEP. As the variable costs start at 0 (no sales = no variable costs) the starting point is the FC line. It then goes diagonally upwards.

☐ The point where the total cost line is crossed by the sales line is the BEP – here sales exceed costs, so you are then into profit.

It will make more sense if you draw one yourself (we'll do this on a spreadsheet shortly). If you draw this really accurately on graph paper you can read off the scale the exact BEP. You can also read off how much profit you can make at different levels of volume.

Activity

Get some graph paper if possible. Otherwise ordinary lined paper will do but just needs a bit more care in measuring and ruling. You'll also need a sharp pencil and a ruler.

Draw a graph using the following data: (It will help if you work out the totals first before you plan your graph.)

Selling price	£12.00
Contribution	25%
Fixed costs	£7,200
Customers	4,000

Spreadsheets

How to do it by hand

1 *Work out the sales.* Customers times selling price (= £48,000).

2 *Work out the contribution.* Sales times CM% (=£12,000).

3 *Work out the variable costs.* Sales less contribution (=£36,000).

4 *Work out the total costs.* Variable plus fixed costs (=£43,200).

5 *Draw the axes for the chart.* On a piece of paper, placed in landscape position, draw a horizontal line about 2cm from the base (the X axis), and a vertical line (for the Y axis) about 2cm from the left edge (so it forms an L shape).

6 *Decide on the scale.* This needs to be enough to accommodate sales of £48,000 on the Y axis and volume of 4,000 on the X axis. Mark off the intermediate points on the scale (say every £5,000 on the Y and every 500 on X). The corner of the L where the X meets the Y is the zero (0) point. Label the axes.

7 *Draw the Sales Line.* Find the point on the top right corner where £48,000 on the Y meets 4,000 on the X. From that point draw a line with a ruler back to 0 (it should look roughly diagonal). Label this line.

8 *Draw the fixed cost line.* Find the point on the Y axis at 0 volume where the costs would equal £7,200. Draw a line horizontal to the X axis at this level (in other words, the end point on the far right is also at £7,200). Label this line also.

9 *Draw the total cost line.* This touches the Y axis at the point where the fixed cost line starts – that is, at £7,200 at 0 volume. It ends on the right side at £43,200 and 4,000 volume. If in doubt look at the BE chart diagram on the previous page. Label this line.

10 *The point where this line crosses the sales line is the break-even point.* Label this point.

11 *Title your chart.*

You may want to offer a discount and need to see the effect on the BEP – in other words, how many more you would need to sell at a reduced price. You can add a new line to your graph for this, and again read off the BEP.

You could also see the effect of putting prices up without raising costs.

How to do a break-even chart on a spreadsheet

This assumes you have already done the exercises above and know a little about the Chart Wizard. This is the data you will need to set up on the spreadsheet:

	A	B	C
1	Data for graph	Start	Finish
2	Sales	0	£48,000
3	Fixed costs	£ 7,200	£ 7,200
4	Total costs	£ 7,200	£43,200

1 *Set up the required data.* On Excel, input the data as above (or use the source data from the question and calculate these out).

2 *Select the data.* Highlight the titles and amounts for Sales, Fixed & Total costs.

3 *Use Chart Wizard.* Insert toolbar, Charts then Line, and choose the first 2D type.

4 *Correct the display.* Click on the chart, to make sure it is still activated, and go to the Design toolbar. Within the Data section, Switch Row/Column.

5 *Add titles.* Type in appropriate titles for chart and axes using Layout, Chart Title, Centred Overlay Title. Then you can do the 2 Axis titles.

6 *Format fonts.* They may be too big to show the scale, depending on the size of your chart. Click on the text you want to change, right-click and select Font.

7 *Notice that the lines do not start at 0 on the Vertical (Y) axis.* Click on the Horizontal (X) axis of the chart ONLY. Layout, Axes, Primary Horizontal Axis then More Primary Horizontal Axis Options. The Vertical Axis should Cross Automatic, and the Position Axis should be On Tick Marks (so click these boxes).

8 *This may be enough.* However, you will notice that the scale on the Horizontal (X) axis is only 1 and 2. If you want to show the full scale for different levels of volume then you need more data. You need to add in data across new columns for each stage of the range that you need – that is for the volume levels 1,000, 2,000, 3,000, 4,000 – see 'Revised data for graph' below. Insert 3 new data columns between the 2 you have already, and enter the new data ranges. To show the scale on the Horizontal axis you need to tell the chart the data that is needed. Click on the chart. Then Design, Data, Select data, then the right box Horizontal (Category) Axis Labels. Click Edit then highlight the data in the Customers row (0-4,000), click OK, then again.

9 *Add an arrow and title to show the BEP.* Click on the chart. Insert a Shape, and choose an arrow. Click on the point where you want to place it. You may need to re-size this arrow if it's too big/small. For the title, Insert a Text Box and type the word 'BEP'. You may need to re-site this using the right-click of your mouse.

Revised data for graph:

Customers	0	1,000	2,000	3,000	4,000
Sales	0	£12,000	£24,000	£36,000	£48,000
Fixed costs	£7,200	£7,200	£7,200	£7,200	£7,200
Total costs	£7,200	£16,200	£25,200	£34,200	£43,200

More charts

Here are some more ideas for charts.

Bar (or column) charts

Most other charts are used to show trends – say in bookings. You've seen how to do a column chart already but you could use a chart to compare actual customers to booked – so you see what proportion are chance guests. If you can do this over a week you could see if there's any difference from day to day.

Table 9.2 shows how it would look – usually boring!

Table 9.2: Customers by day

Day	Booked	Chance	Total
Monday	2	8	10
Tuesday	2	10	12
Wednesday	6	14	20
Thursday	10	14	24
Friday	30	20	50
Saturday	45	15	60
Sunday	10	10	20

Here it's better to use a stacked column or bar chart.

Activity

If you have access to a spreadsheet, try doing the above table in a bar-chart format. If you type in the information exactly as above you can then use that for your source data for Chart Wizard (or similar in non-Excel spreadsheets). See how much more interesting it looks. If you can do this over a period of weeks and see some real trends then you may be able to use it to decide how you approach the problem of bookings.

Line charts

These can also be used, as well as for break-even, for displaying sales levels by day or by month. You could use different lines for different departments, or compare year-to-year for a meeting presentation. They can be used to show staffing levels in different months. Trying to describe these can be difficult – a picture (that is, chart) is far more effective.

Activity   Using the Total Customers data only from the table above, practise doing a line chart.

More practice on spreadsheets

Setting up a spreadsheet for your own personal cash flow practises a range of techniques. Write down all your money coming in and going out, then try and set up a spreadsheet in the style of the cash forecast that was covered in Chapter 6. You could also draw a chart to show the surplus or deficit – what sort of chart would be good for this?

Here's the sort of things you might need:

Cash in	Wages (net), Rent from lodger
Cash out	Rent or mortgage, Food, Travel to work, Household bills, Clothes, Entertainment, Savings for holiday

Don't forget you'll also need to know what you have in the bank already.

Summary

In this chapter we have looked at how we can use spreadsheets for management tasks and discussed a range of techniques to improve our skills.

You have:

- Discussed a range of design techniques to assist in the effective construction of a spreadsheet
- Practised exercises to aid in the development of skills
- Discussed a range of scenarios where spreadsheets might be used
- Discussed the use of charts to aid in decision making
- Practised chart construction by spreadsheet and by hand.

Spreadsheets

10 Being part of a company

- Features of the industry
- Theft
- Stakeholders
- Organisation
- Accounts

Introduction

Some of you may work in a very small business, where you know the owner and everybody else in the organisation. The majority of the businesses in hospitality are small – pubs, restaurants, cafes, visitor attractions and so on.

But for others, you may feel that you are a very small part of a very large organisation. Some hospitality companies are enormous – and may well be part of an even larger conglomerate (a multi-industry, multinational corporation). Businesses change ownership frequently – some of the big names of five years ago are no longer around in the same way, and other previously small names are now big ones.

Whatever the size of the business, you do count, and in this chapter we want to show you how you fit into the larger organisation – whether for now or for the future. We will look at the types of ownership and then the structure of companies and the type of accounts that they do. Later on we will consider two other ways that businesses can operate – under franchise and by management contract – where the building is owned by one entity but run by another.

By the end of this chapter, therefore, you should be able to:

- Distinguish between the different types of company ownership
- Describe the basic format of a company report
- Describe the differences between a franchise and a management contract.

Ownership of business

There are three basic types of ownership – sole trader, partnership and limited company. We will look at each in turn, describe the features and then look at the type of reports they have to produce by law. For the sole trader and partnership these are fairly simple but limited companies (which are generally much larger) have complex reports to produce.

Sole trader

This is one person in business who owns a pub, cafe, shop or similar and probably employs staff to work for them. Maybe you work for one of these. Legally the owner is fully responsible for all the activities of the business – and all the profits or losses. So, if the business fails, they are personally liable for the debts. It's not unusual, therefore, for the sole trader to have very few personal assets – the house, car, personal bank account and so on may all be held in their spouse or partner's name. This may sound rather unethical, but it is legal.

Sole traders generally do all their own business accounts, which they need to keep separate from their personal accounts, and then pay income tax on any profits. They have to keep records but these can be fairly simple – records of all revenue and expenditure – and so a simple profit and loss (P&L) and balance sheet (BS) are adequate. One extra item you may see on the balance sheet in the 'financed by' section is 'drawings' which are monies taken out of the business by the owner as profits. These are shown separately to ensure that too much money isn't being extracted when the business can't afford it.

It's advisable to have the accounts formally reviewed by a qualified accountant once a year as they can help reduce the tax, and Revenue and Customs are less likely to query things if the accounts have been independently checked.

So, there are advantages and disadvantages of sole trader status:

For	Simple accounts
	Keep the business under your own control
	Keep it small and manageable
	Plenty of time to pay tax
Against	Personally liable for debts
	Lack of opportunity to expand as you're limited by your own funds (and any the bank will lend you)

Partnership

In a partnership two or more people go into business together. They don't have to be equal partners – one can own a greater percentage then the other(s). Often the percentage ownership is based on the amount of capital (initial money) invested in the business at the beginning, but this isn't always true. For instance, parents may invest in a pub which their children run – but all remain equal partners. One invests money, the other skills and time. There can be some very big partnerships although generally you are not allowed to have more than 20. The majority of hospitality, tourism and leisure businesses are small and are owned and run by either a partnership or sole trader.

Legally all partners are responsible for the running of the business – and so for profits or losses. Any profits are shared out according to the partnership agreement that, by law, they all have to sign (this contract also includes lots of other items such as what to do if they fall out, or decide to close the business). If the business fails then they are personally liable for the losses.

Companies

The way in which they prepare their accounts is a little more complicated than for a sole trader. Once the P&L has been calculated down to the net profit line then an extra section is added – the appropriation account. This is where the profits are 'appropriated' (allocated, or portioned out) to the partners. The partners pay income tax on their part of the profits. If the partners shared profits equally then the Appropriation Account would look like this:

Net profit			£20,000
Appropriated:	Partner 1	50%	£10,000
	Partner 2	50%	£10,000

The BS has sub-sections in the 'Financed By' section which shows each partner's capital account and current account where their shares of the initial investment and profits are held. Again this is obviously a simple generalisation – an accountant is best qualified to advise you properly here. Tax-wise, each partner is responsible for the tax on their own share of the business. So, the advantages and disadvantages of partnership status are:

For	Fairly simple accounts
	Keep the business under control of the partners but with additional expertise from each partner
	Easier to expand if you all want to
Against	Still personally liable for debts
	Sharing the business means sharing profits, but also losses
	Potential for disagreement

Limited liability companies

This is the way that you reduce your liability for the debts of the company – while still sharing in the profits. Companies can be very small or multinational giants. There are two types of limited company – private and public. If you invest in one of these your financial liability is limited to the amount you originally put in – you are not personally liable for the debts of the company.

The capital of the company (what was the Financed By section before) is divided – or shared out – into millions (usually) of small, equal portions called shares. The way that you own part of the company is to own a proportion of the shares – of which more detail later. However, you as an individual may only be able to influence the management of the company if you are a director or very senior executive.

LTDs and LLPs

Private limited companies (usually abbreviated to Ltd) have shares that can be only owned by a restricted band of people – usually the original family owners and employees of the company. Ltds often emerge from partnerships, when the owners decide that they want to keep the business separate from their personal affairs and reduce their financial liability in the case of loss.

There's another form of Ltd company called a Limited Liability Partnership (LLP) which is run like a partnership but has a separate legal entity and so has limited liability for debts. This is popular amongst professional service firms such as accountants and solicitors.

PLCs

Public limited companies (PLCs) have shares that can be bought and sold by anybody via the Stock Exchange (there's a bit more about the Stock Market further on in this chapter). The advantages and disadvantages of a business being part of a company are:

For	Shareholder's liability for debt is limited to the amount they invest
	Opportunity to raise funds from lots of sources
	Lots of expertise available from a range of people
	Easier to expand if the directors wish to
Against	Complex accounts
	Lack of control by individuals
	Have to share the profits with investors

We will go through the format of their accounts after we have considered how you might fit into the structure of a company. First, Figure 10.1 shows a simplified flow chart for a contract catering division to illustrate how the whole company is structured, from individual unit (where you might work) to the total corporation.

The divisions or sections themselves may be registered as individual companies, usually wholly or substantially owned by the parent company, for tax or operational reasons.

Companies

Activity	Do you know which type of business you belong to? If it's a large one do you know what all the other divisions do?

Figure 10.1: Company structure

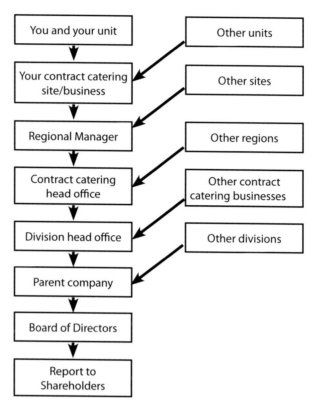

Aspects of company accounts

As mentioned in Chapter 2, businesses have two types of accounts – management accounts and published accounts.

Management accounts are those that are used within the business and utilise the P&L and BS structures that we've used in earlier chapters. These are designed for the managers to help them run the business more effectively. You'll normally have one set of management accounts for each unit, and a summary for the overall business.

Published accounts are a legal requirement for limited companies and they are also designed for the shareholders, the investors and any other stakeholders – people who have an interest in how the company operates. This could include you!

The structure is formally specified so that many elements of all published accounts look the same. They are contained in the Annual Report, a glossy publication – either print and/or web-based – that also includes various other statements and statistics for the financial year. There are also interim reports that are a brief summary of the half-yearly or quarterly results.

Activity	Please go to your company website – or another that interests you – and download a copy of the Annual Report (usually in PDF format). You can also access these from financial websites, but may have to pay a fee. Look at the content. Now let's 'walk through' and see what's in it.

Content of the Annual Report

Chairman's (or Chief Executive Officer's) statement

This tends to be as glossy as the report style! They obviously try to make the company look as good as possible, so if it's been a bad year they'll talk about 'challenges' and how things are now improving. You need to study the contents of the entire report to see how open they've been about what has happened.

A good CEO or chairman will also thank the employees for their contribution to the company success. You'll often also read about the company's attitude towards their various stakeholders (employees, community, the environment).

Finance Director's statement

This focuses specifically on the financial performance of the company and will include some key ratios.

List of directors

This usually has a brief profile of who they are.

Directors' emoluments

This is what they have been paid – and not just in money but also in share options, bonuses and benefits (the whole package can be *enormous*).

Profit & Loss statement

This is shown below and is a little different from the structure we're used to. You'll also see a number in a column (often in italics) – this relates to the 'Notes to the Accounts' where you'll find lots of detail as to what makes up the particular line. You will also see two years' figures – the immediate past year and the one before that. You may also see a summary statement for five years.

Balance sheet

Again, this is a bit different in layout and also has two years' figures.

Cash flow

This shows where the money has come from and gone to. It details all revenues, not just from sales but also from investments and interest pay-

Companies

ments. Some cash is tied up in stocks and debtors, other cash goes out to pay shareholders their profits (dividends) and to pay debts.

If you want to read more about the Cash Flow statement then see the reading list at the end of the book.

Notes to the accounts

These are *really* useful because they contain lots of information about the company (such as number of employees, major shareholders, debts and so on) that can't be shown on the P&L and BS. The number on the note is the reference number from the P&L or BS.

Why reports are useful to you

They can tell you a lot about the company. By carefully reading all the detail, and perhaps looking at a few ratios (more below), you can find out what their attitudes are and how successful they are in their various enterprises. What you might want to look at:

☐ The turnover (revenue or 'income'). How does it compare to previous years? Are they doing better or worse?

☐ The profits. Are they growing? Think about why that would be. It can be good or bad depending on your viewpoint.

☐ Staffing costs and average wage costs (low wages might = high profits). Does the company talk about investing in its workforce? Do they pay pensions and offer training and development?

☐ The directors' salaries – are they worth it? How does this compare to the average wage cost?

☐ Whether the company is growing in size, and hopefully without too much growth of debts.

☐ Where they stand on ethical issues. Do they invest in environmentally sound projects and practices?

☐ Whether they're investing for the future – in staff, in equipment, in technology.

☐ Who owns the company?

☐ Whether ownership is in the hands of a few large stockholders.

Activity Suppose your business was bought by another company which doesn't have a good environmental record? Or perhaps they've been 'outed' for unethical practices, or employing child labour in a Third World country. How do you react?

Published Profit and Loss report

This is the one found in the annual report.

To the right you'll see columns for the two years' trading and also the reference number for the Notes to the Accounts. Here is a very simplified explanation of the layout as there can be further data relating to other businesses that form part of the company.

Turnover (continuing operations) This is revenue received from day-to-day trading

Less cost of sales This isn't the same as you are used to. It means *all* costs (including labour) except administrative and selling costs

= *Gross profit* So this isn't the same as the GP shown in management accounts

Less net operating expenses This is the selling and administrative expenses

= *Operating profit*

Plus or minus profit/loss on sale of property and other fixed assets If you sell a property or other fixed asset you may make a loss or profit

= *Profit before interest*

Less net interest payable Interest on loans that you have to pay

= *Profit before taxation*

Less tax on profit from ordinary activities The Corporation Tax payable on these profits

= *Profit after taxation*

Less Dividends paid This is the way that profits are shared out amongst the shareholders – see below when we discuss types of shares

= *Retained profit* This is the money kept back in the company for re-investment in the business

Activity

You could compare this to the annual report that you have and see what it contains. The Notes will help you decipher the various entries. Are there other items that appear? Do you know what they all mean? If necessary find a textbook (see the reading list) and look up the terminology. If you see a column headed 'exceptional items' then it's likely that the company bought or sold a substantial section of business. By showing these separately the reader can concentrate on the part of the business that continues into the next year, and make comparisons to other years, and to other investments.

Companies

Published balance sheet

Fixed assets

> *Tangible*   These are things you can touch – buildings, equipment and so on
>
> *Intangible*   Goodwill, brand names
>
> *Investments*   These are money invested in other companies which is long-term and unlikely to change daily

Plus current assets

> *Stocks*   These are all the same as an internal BS that you are familiar with
> *Debtors*
>
> *Bank*
>
> *Prepayments*

Less creditors due within one year

> *Interest payable*   These are all short-term (current) liabilities
>
> *Tax payable*
>
> *Dividend payable*
>
> *Creditors due within one year*
>
> *Accruals*

= Net current assets

> *Less: Creditors due after one year (also called 'debt')*   Other debts due for repayment over a year, including debentures which are a form of loan

= Total net assets

> This is the balancing (total) figure

Shareholders funds (also called 'equity')

> These are the monies that belong to the shareholders
>
> *Called-up share capital*   The original value of the shares (*not* what's being quoted on the stock market)
>
> *Reserves*   Money put aside for refurbishment in the future and also retained for future expansion
>
> *Profit & Loss account*   Profits earned by the company that belong to the owners – the shareholders

=Total capital and reserves

> The other balancing figure

Activity	Again, look at 'your' report and see what's in it.

Shares

The capital of a company is divided into lots of equal shares that have a 'nominal' or face value. These are then sold to the general public (and to banks, pension funds, investment trusts and other large investors) at a higher price and the difference between the selling price and the nominal value is the 'share premium'. As a shareholder you are paid your proportion of the profits in the form of a dividend.

There are two main types of shares – *preference* and *ordinary*.

Preference shares

The reason that they are 'preferred' is because:

☐ The dividend is paid first

☐ In the event of liquidation, the preference shareholders are repaid before other shareholders.

These shares carry a fixed rate of dividend which is expressed as a percentage of the nominal value so, for instance, a £1 (nominal value) 9% preference share would earn 9 pence dividend per year. This payment doesn't change whether it is a good year or not.

Ordinary shares

The ordinary shareholders bear the greatest risk because

☐ Their dividend is only paid when there are enough profits, although if profits are good then they may earn high dividends

☐ They are last in line for repayment if the company fails (after everybody else).

Dividends are paid in 'pence per share'.

How to calculate dividends:

Preference shares are paid in two parts and are called *interim* (half-year) and *final* (year-end).

Example: 9% preference share dividend for 1,000 × £1 shares

Interim	4.5% × £1	4.5 pence	× 1,000	= £45
Final	4.5% × £1	4.5 pence	× 1,000	= £45
			Total paid	= £90

Ordinary shares earn a different amount according to the profits available.

Example: £1 shares – half-year profits good so interim dividend high at 10p/share. Final profits are less good so dividend lower at 6p/share, for 1,000 shares

Interim	10 pence	× 1,000	= £100
Final	6 pence	× 1,000	= £ 60
		Total paid	= £160

Ratios that can be calculated

In addition to the ratios that we've covered in other chapters there are a few that you can do on published accounts too. Some of these will be stated in the annual report – others you may need to work out yourself (or you may be able to access them via financial websites – see the reading list).

They can help you understand more about how the company is performing. Remember, though, that what's a 'good' ratio for one person may be 'bad' for another. For instance, a high profit percentage may be good for shareholders (more dividends) but mean a lower wage percentage (bad for employees) although usually it is good for both because a successful company can, in theory, afford to pay higher rates. Employees may also benefit from company share options – which can be a profitable way for staff to have a financial interest in their company without having to find cash to invest by themselves.

$$\text{Return on ordinary shareholders funds} \quad = \quad \frac{\text{Profit after tax \& pref. Share dividend £}}{\text{Ordinary shareholders funds £}} \, \%$$

This is the percentage return that ordinary shareholders may see from profits. It isn't the same as dividends because it's calculated for the year on the profit from the previous year, before profit is retained in the business.

$$\text{Return on capital employed (ROCE)} \quad = \quad \frac{\text{Profit before interest \& tax £}}{\text{Shareholders' funds + Long-term debt £}} \, \%$$

The capital employed is the debt and equity together – so all the long-term liabilities. ROCE means the percentage profit compared to these long-term liabilities.

$$\text{Earnings per share (in pence) (EPS)} \quad = \quad \frac{\text{Profit after tax \& preference share dividend £}}{\text{Number of issued ordinary shares}}$$

This is how much money is earned in profits on average by each share. Again, it's not the actual dividend figure because it's calculated before reserves are extracted.

$$\text{Price/earnings ratio (P/E)} \quad = \quad \frac{\text{Market price per share £}}{\text{Earnings per share £}}$$

We've talked about the 'nominal value' of the shares before, but they can be bought and sold on the stock market at whatever price people are willing to pay (the 'market price' of the shares). The price is based on predictions of profits (and hence dividends) and the growth of the company, so the higher the market price, the more desirable they are. The P/E ratio measures the market price against the EPS.

$$\text{Gearing} = \frac{\text{Long-term loans + pref shares + short-term debt £}}{\text{Ordinary shares \& reserves £}}$$

Gearing is the relationship between debt (money borrowed) to equity (shareholders' funds). Generally, the lower the gearing (less debt to equity) then the more stable the company is. A company that is 'highly geared' has borrowed a lot of money to expand, which isn't a problem for as long as the lending institutions (banks etc.) still trust you, and you have enough cash to pay the interest due on the debt. If the trust is destroyed then the banks may 'call in' their debts which can often mean the collapse of the company.

Here is an example of gearing:

Two Companies – Alpha and Beta

	Alpha (£000)	Beta (£000)	
Issued share capital			
50p Ordinary shares	300	450	*Equity*
10% Preference shares	225		*Debt*
Reserves			
Revaluation reserve	105	150	*Equity*
Retained earnings	225	300	*Equity*
Loan capital			
8% Debentures	450	225	Debt
10% Debentures			Debt

Calculation of gearing

(Formula is total debt divided by total equity expressed as a percentage)

	Alpha (£000)	Beta (£000)
Sources	$\dfrac{450+225}{300+105+225}$	$\dfrac{225}{450+150+300}$
=	$\dfrac{675}{630}$	$\dfrac{225}{900}$
=	107%	25%

Look at the amount to debt to repay. Alpha has a very high gearing (lots of debt) and so is vulnerable if the banks and other lending institutions were to lose confidence. Beta has very low gearing and could (and should) borrow money for expansion if they have a profitable product or service, for which there is a thriving market.

Companies

Exercise 10.1

Here's a small exercise for you to calculate some ratios, based on the above and any others that you can remember that have already been covered.

Profit & Loss Account	£000s	Balance Sheet	£000s
Turnover	1,875	**Fixed assets**	
- Cost of sales	(1,410)	Tangible	510
= Gross profit	465	**Current assets**	
- Operating expenses	(190)	Stocks	375
= Profit before interest and tax	275	Debtors	250
- Interest	(25)	Cash & short-term deposits	60
= Profit before tax	250	= total	685
- Tax	(82)	Creditors within one year	
= Profit after tax	168	Bank and other borrowings	(437)
Dividends	(100)	Net current assets	248
= Retained profit for year	68	Total assets less current liabilities	758
		Creditors due after one year	
		Bank and other borrowings	(340)
		= Net Assets employed	418
		Capital & reserves	
		Called-up share capital	250
		Profit & Loss account (profit after tax)	168
		Equity shareholders funds	418

Assume that the market price per share is £1.50, and that there are 500,000 shares. You are asked to calculate appropriate ratios (please don't forget there are others we did in earlier chapters too).

You will find the answers at the end of the book.

Tip

Work out the nominal (issue) price of the shares first by taking the called-up share capital, divided by the number of shares.

Are these results good or bad? What was the market share compared to its nominal value? What does this tell you about the 'market view' of this company? Think about what these numbers are telling you.

Activity

Please get a copy of a quality newspaper ('broadsheet' not tabloid) and go to the financial pages, or look on their website. Look at the prices quoted for various companies – it doesn't have to be in the hospitality or tourism sector. Then look at some of the comments made in other sections. The most useful company to look at in depth is one that is 'publishing' its results that day, so that there is a critique from a range of financial commentators.

Share ownership

Existing companies

These are already quoted on the Stock Exchange. There are two prices quoted – *buy* and *sell*. Transactions are made through 'brokers' who will obtain the best market price that they can, and take a commission on the sale. Once sold; the actual transfer of shares and cash takes place five days after sale is made. Anybody over 18 with the necessary cash can do it!

A *bull market* is optimistic, where there are generally more investors wanting to purchase shares than there are willing sellers, because of a positive outlook for company performance and profitability.

A *bear market* is pessimistic, where there are generally more investors wanting to sell shares than there are purchasers, because of a negative outlook on company performance and profitability.

If you want to read up more about how the stock market works, then please see the reading list.

New companies

If you want to buy shares in a brand new company that hasn't yet been trading on the stock market (although they will probably have been in business as an Ltd or partnership for some time) then you will see an 'Offer for Sale' when they 'go public'. You apply to buy a certain number of shares. Depending on how well-subscribed they are (that is, how popular) you may or may not get all the shares you ask for.

Although shares are issued at their *nominal* (or face) value you will probably have to pay a *premium* which is an additional amount. The higher the potential demand for shares, the higher the premium. For instance, two companies going public each with £1 (nominal) shares to offer:

☐ Company A is profitable, innovative and has identified a niche market and so potentially will make large profits. Its £1 shares are offered at £3.50 (a premium of £2.50) which reflects the demand and potential profits.

☐ Company B is also profitable (otherwise it wouldn't be going public) but isn't as fashionable as Company A, and so the future predictions aren't as good. Its £1 shares are offered at £1.50 (a premium of only £0.50) which reflects the reduced demand.

Companies

Franchising and management contracts

Some companies both own and operate properties under their own name. However, often companies wish to separate ownership from operations. The solution is to either use a well-known brand name for their properties or to just operate with another company owning the property. One approach is franchising and another is management contracting and the two are fairly similar in concept although with different modes of operation.

Franchising

Franchising occurs when an owner (usually of property but sometimes just of staff and skills) decides to go into business and use the expertise of an established operator. Typically this will be an established brand name with a standard product. This is one of the few ways that a small operator can enter the larger market. They take on a licence for a particular area and operate the business.

Examples of franchises in hospitality are pizza restaurants, fast-food takeaways and hotel groups. A hotel group looking to franchise will typically have many hotels that they wish to operate under their own control but with a proven brand name. The operator stays in control – it is *their* business.

Advantages of being a franchisee are:

☐ Availability of a new market with a proven brand name

☐ Assistance in finding a site, and exclusive trading within a given area (so the franchiser won't grant any more licences within your 'patch')

☐ Assistance in planning the layout of the property (if used – you can franchise a window cleaning business, for instance)

☐ Advice on all aspects of the business

☐ Training of core management staff

☐ Menus and recipes if required

☐ Supplies of branded products (soap, paper napkins, etc.)

☐ Advertising and promotion on a national level.

Advantages to the franchisor (the owner of the brand) are:

☐ The opportunity to expand their business with little capital.

☐ The opportunity to receive a fee or 'royalty' of a percentage of the sales, plus often a set fee for the other services

☐ Exposure in a much wider market (it's called 'market penetration')

☐ The ability to keep their own core operation (head office) compact whilst still providing extensive services.

There are also benefits to the customer as they see a proven brand name but with the comfort of having an operator who knows the local market and hence local needs. The only disadvantage to franchisors and franchisees is the dependence on each other and hence potential for problems if either fails to keep their side of the agreement.

Management contracts

These are used where the owner of the brand wishes to continue to operate their businesses and expand their name and business without a major capital investment. Typically a property company will own the actual building but they are not interested in running the business themselves (unlike a franchise). They will ask someone else to do it for them by hiring a management company to run the business under their established name. This is most common in hotels – many of the major international groups operate in this way.

The advantages to the operator are:

☐ Expansion (often globally) of the brand – again it's market penetration

☐ A large number of properties where managers can be placed and then train the local workforce in the company standards

☐ As a result improved (international ?) career opportunities for staff

☐ Formulation of accounts based on the USALI (see Chapter 2) – for standardisation and benchmarking

☐ Receipt of fees, often based both on a percentage of sales and on a percentage of profits

☐ The ability to influence local trade without major financial investment

☐ The owner provides funds for all capital investment and for working capital, so there is limited financial outlay

☐ A fixed time period for operation – often five years.

The advantages to the owner of the property are:

☐ The benefit of a known brand

☐ The benefit of trained management and standardised systems

☐ A guarantee of maintenance of standards

☐ An income with minimal effort but with major investment (they provide the building, fixtures and fittings, equipment and working capital)

☐ Standard reporting of profits using the USALI for consistency.

There have been several examples where hotel groups have entered into joint ventures to own properties with other partners, often in countries with a previous lack of investment and/or hotel infrastructure. For instance, in some 'developing' countries major groups linked with local property owners and governments as joint partners. Here there may have been a lack of investment which, when coupled with a growing market, creates the opportunity for development. The initial investment by the management company guarantees their interest and commitment to making the contract work (they're not going to pull out after a year if the business is unsuccessful). Typically after several years as joint owners the hotel group will sell out to the other partners or to commercial investors, but continue to manage the property on an ongoing basis.

One other area where the management contract approach has been used is for hotels or restaurants in receivership. The property will then be 'owned' by a bank or financial institution as a result of the original owners going bankrupt. As a going concern the business is more likely to be sold and also is less likely to deteriorate so the new owner may well want to keep the business running. In this case a small management contractor (perhaps even a management consultant) may be asked to operate the business, usually without a standard brand name and for a limited period of time.

Summary

In this chapter we have reviewed the structure of companies and hopefully helped you to visualise where you might fit as part of the 'bigger picture'. We've looked at the structure of annual reports and identified some ratios that can be used to analyse these. The later part of the chapter described franchises and management contracts. Hence you are now able to:

- Identify the differences between the three types of business ownership – sole trader, partnership and limited company

- Describe the main features of an annual report

- Analyse ratios relevant to published accounts

- Identify the differences between management contracts and franchises.

11 Conclusions and developing your skills

- Anticipating trends
- Developing your financial skills further
- Looking after your staff

Introduction

In this chapter we will look at using the information from this book to help you develop further as a manager and consider how to look ahead, not just by forecasting but by predicting trends and so identifying how you can best use this to your advantage.

By improving your own skills as a manager, in the future you will be well equipped to take advantage of all the opportunities available to you. This will include looking at the types of training and education that you can undertake, and other areas that might be useful. Although professional development may not be immediately obvious as a finance topic it's relevant to all of us – and financial management is a key skill for all hospitality managers now.

By the end of this chapter you will be able to:

- ■ Collate the various themes of this book
- ■ Be aware of trends in the industry
- ■ Identify some of the other resources available to help you develop your skills.

Key themes

So, what have you learned from this book?

☐ The importance of maximising revenue in order to optimise profits or achieve BEP. A combination of control, accurate pricing and marketing is needed, and ratios are invaluable in helping identify areas for action.

☐ The importance of controlling costs and stocks without affecting customer service – so you need to optimise rather than minimise these. Different types of costs are found in different sectors, and in fact some units or departments have only costs and not revenues. Where there are very tight margins the control of costs is paramount to achieve business objectives – small variances, and small actions (such as the slice of tomato) can make big differences overall. Being able to identify where the differences are by using ratios and standard costing techniques is essential to profitability (or BEP).

☐ Attitudes of managers are crucial. If you 'lead from the top' and make it clear that wastage and theft are unacceptable then half the battle is won. Most staff are intrinsically honest, but sloppy and/or dishonest leadership can make them careless too. Walking the job ('MBWA') is one of the best ways to identify problems, especially when used in conjunction with ratio analysis.

☐ Planning all aspects of the business helps managers in a variety of ways. Forecasting customer levels and use of standard costing techniques allows planning of purchasing and staffing which minimises wastage and hence costs. Planning the control of all areas helps you anticipate potential problems before they occur and the use of spreadsheets is vital in achieving accurate results.

☐ Cash and stocks are very desirable and so need strong controls at all stages of the working capital cycle. Forecasting cash requirements is helpful to the business, but nothing beats simple effective systems and a good lock with minimal distribution of keys.

☐ Decisions made at unit level impact at higher levels of the organisation. Some management reports are designed for use by managers within their own areas, others for the general manager or owner. If you are part of a larger organisation then your unit report will be amalgamated with others to produce overall company reports. These are then converted into a different structure for publication in an annual report that addresses the needs of the various stakeholders.

☐ The customer always comes first.

Anticipating trends

A key to your successful career in the future will be your ability to forecast trends. You may think you are a small fish in a big pond, but hopefully you'll grow into a bigger fish (which may be one reason why you are reading this).

We've been looking at your current level of operation, mostly from a short-term perspective. It's important, though, to also look strategically – a long way ahead. You need to try and anticipate how the business where you work (either now or in the future) will grow, and then whether you will be a part of that. Many of the techniques we've learned can help you because by tracking what has happened you can make some predictions for the future.

For instance, if you see that revenues are growing and the company is buying more businesses, then the chances are that your career will grow too. On the other hand, if the business is struggling then you might want to start considering your next career move. Below are some things to look out for. You should remember that, although these examples don't appear to be directly financial in nature, all activities have a financial impact on the business in one way or another.

Developing skills

☐ Growth in hospitality and tourism as a whole

☐ Changes in the national economy which affect visitors from overseas

☐ Incidents or events that affect tourism (and hence most hospitality businesses) – such as volcanic ash clouds, a terrorist attack or major sporting events. These may be local, national or international.

☐ Trends in eating out

☐ Trends in regional and local business, such as new hotels, hospitals, visitor attractions

☐ Anything happening in your sector

☐ Anything happening in your company or organisation.

How do you find these out? – by reading (see below), listening, watching, going to places and general participation in the activities of your operation and the industry (and perhaps your professional association too). There also some websites listed at the back of the book.

Developing your financial skills further

Now that you have reviewed what you have learned, what next? Practise!

Hopefully having worked your way through this book you'll have been able to learn new techniques and practise a range of skills. You can use them in the workplace in all sorts of ways to really help you become a better supervisor or manager. It obviously depends on how much financial information is available to you – the attitude of senior management can vary – but by being proactive you'll be able to make progress to a real understanding of the financial relevance of what you do.

Here are some suggestions:

☐ If you have financial statements then ask to see them each month. Look at the actual against budget for both revenues and costs, and see if you can identify what's working well and what isn't. Can you identify why things have happened? If it's good you could do it again, if it isn't so good, can you fix it?

☐ You could calculate ratios if they're not already done. Is there a relationship between volume and price? If sales have fallen, have costs fallen too? Which costs are fixed, and which are variable?

☐ Next time something needs pricing, or costing, could you help?

☐ Compare a budgeted recipe cost to the actual. Are there any variances and, if so, why?

☐ Do a forecast of customers, and see how it impacts on other areas.

☐ Look at other businesses as a customer yourself, and learn from them – both what they are doing well and what they're falling behind on. Sometimes you can be more objective looking at an operation that isn't your own, where you don't know the people or the quirks of the operation (and so don't make excuses for them).

Further resources

Internet

There are lots of websites that can help you find a variety of sources of information. A selection are listed at the end of this book. For example:

☐ Trade and professional associations

☐ Government sites, including education links

☐ Training and careers advice

☐ Networking links.

Magazines and journals

Trade magazines, such as *Caterer and Hotelkeeper*, are one of the best ways to keep up to date because they talk about what's happening now. They do report on day-to-day activities and there will be one at least (and probably more) that focus on your sector. The professional associations also all have their own journals or newsletters. You get a lot of opinions in the trade press and not everybody agrees with these!

Reports

Several organisations provide detailed statistical analysis and commentary on industry trends, from regional hotels to world tourism and from employment statistics to trends in eating out – please see the list of websites.

Books (like this one)

At the end of this book there are a range of books quoted, but there are a lot more that may be helpful too. This is just a personal selection that matches with the topics we've discussed but you may well find many others that you prefer.

Using books can be a major help in developing your skills, so if you don't get on with a particular writer please try others. Different books suit different people – some people like a very technical style, others prefer a more user-friendly approach – it's all a matter of taste. If you aren't technically minded then books written for non-specialists may be best for you

Developing skills

– for example if you want more on finance then a book titled 'finance for non-financial managers' or similar will be written in a non-expert style.

Where to find books

When you've decided the sort of information that you want to find out then it's a case of going to look at what's available.

University and college libraries

They will usually let you go in and look at books ('for reference') although you won't be able to borrow them unless you are a registered student. It's worth checking first, though, that they do offer hospitality courses. The more courses they offer (and the higher the level) the greater the range of books, journals, reports and trade magazines they are likely to have.

Local libraries

The range of hospitality books will be minimal (if any) so you need to look at the business studies areas. They tend to stock 'beginner-level' books which assume that you are 'intelligent but uninformed'. Local libraries are excellent for careers and education information, both local and national. They may also offer Internet access to wider resources.

Institute of Hospitality

They have a library that you can go and visit if you are a member. It's worth checking what they have in a particular topic area before you go, though. They will also send you things by mail although return postage can be expensive. They also have a lot of e-books that you can access on request.

Bookshops

Academic bookshops stock a reasonable range of books and can order for you if you wish. You can always go in and 'thumb the shelves' although again their range may be limited if they are not a hospitality specialist. Ordinary bookshops tend to just have general business-type books.

Online

You could look at publishers' websites (the reading lists in this book give you their details) and see their profiles of their various publications, including sections from chapters. You may be able to buy direct at a discount, or via Internet bookshops (where you may be also be able to look at the – limited – descriptions of books that are available).

Developing your skills

You need to get as much training and education as you can! It extends your skills, gives you perspective and helps you understand how other areas and people 'tick'. Although we're concentrating on finance this is important for other areas too. Training and education can be in-company or independent. You can often persuade employers to pay for development that is generally in your area of work although they are more likely to pay for short courses than long ones (such as a Master's course that is very expensive). You may be able to borrow money to study (see the Directgov website in the resources list).

Anything to help your self-development is good – and that can mean non-hospitality things too. The important thing is that you learn and then promote that learning on your CV. So, for example, drama classes aren't just about having fun. They develop your self-confidence, your ability to speak in public, to think on your feet and to present to an audience.

Some educational courses earn you qualifications, others just develop your skills. Here are some ideas:

Local authority evening (or day) classes

These tend to run in school terms. You can study a wide range of skills, some that will result in qualifications, some not. You may have to do quite a bit of studying in your own time. There are some in hospitality, but any business studies area would be useful too.

Certificate and diploma courses

These tend to be vocational – focusing on skills rather than management approaches. They are usually run in local further education colleges. You may be able to study full time, part time or at a distance, or day-release from work. Some professional associations such as BAHA (the British Association of Hospitality Accountants – see the website address) run their own courses.

Degree courses

These are run by universities and some colleges. You may have to study full time, which would mean you concentrating on education for a few years, rather than work (though you may be able to work part time). You can usually get a student loan to pay your fees but you still have to find a lot of extra cash to fund this. You may also be able to study at a distance or online with organisations such as the Open University.

Developing skills

Master's level

This is postgraduate level study. You don't necessarily need an undergraduate degree to study at this level as some universities have an open-entry approach which means that you can join providing you have sufficient management experience – usually two or three years. You'll find it tough at first, but the rewards can be enormous. Several universities (including, of course, the Open University) now offer courses via on-line learning. Learning by yourself can be lonely and time-consuming, so make sure it suits you before you sign up.

Financial skills

Have you 'got the bug'? If you enjoy finance then you may want to develop your skills in this area a bit more (or lots more).

If you just want to be more financially competent then reading more in the area will help (as shown above). You can also study short courses locally – see above – or for basic generic qualifications such as AAT (Association of Accounting Technicians).

If you really think you like numbers – and as we've seen it's a lot about logic and being able to use a calculator, rather than an ability to do mathematics – then you could consider more formal financial training. BAHA runs courses for people wishing to develop their skills. Their finance qualifications give you some exemptions from CIMA (Chartered Institute of Management Accountants) examinations, which are the more formal accounting qualifications probably best suited for practising financial managers. They also offer courses in revenue management and information technology.

BAHA is also a good source of information about hospitality financial management issues and also holds meetings both regionally and in London, where you can meet with other financial professionals from the industry.

The Institute of Hospitality has a similar approach and, being much larger, has frequent events within each local area.

Careers in finance

If you enjoy working with numbers then could you think about working in an accounts office? You don't have to do all the accountancy exams if you don't want to, as there are lots of opportunities for people in different areas of control that don't require a lot of formal qualifications.

Looking after your staff

Finally – one of the common themes in the hospitality industry is that it is all about people. It's not just numbers – people are crucial to the industry both as customers and as employees. It makes sense, therefore, to look after them.

The main problems from a control aspect are theft and wastage and effective management of these is dependent on effective management of your customers and, most importantly, the staff who work with you. Accurate systems and physical controls are important but it is people who use these.

For you to be an effective manager means developing a culture of trust and integrity by leading from the top – if you are honest then they will be too. If they are trusted to behave honestly and professionally then effective controls will happen and the result will be a profitable business.

Last, please recognise achievements – notice things that are working well as well as those that aren't. Praise is crucial to all of us, whether formal through appraisal or informal via a 'pat on the back'. Look after your staff and they'll make your job easier in return. A last mini-case for you:

Mini-case

The department had been enormously busy and the workload had been made worse as two staff were off – one on holiday and another on maternity leave.

Most staff had worked extra time to help out but weren't entitled to overtime payments. The manager could have made a case to pay everybody a small bonus, but they would have forgotten about it in a couple of days (and would have had to pay tax on it).

Instead she went out and bought each person a big box of very good chocolates as a present. This made an immediate difference to morale – the staff knew that she'd taken trouble to do this and that this meant she cared about them and recognised that they did a good job. Although they were all still tired they were able to see that the overload would soon be at an end.

This does show you that pay isn't the only motivator, or even the most effective – often it's how you behave and care about your staff that matters.

Glossary

ADV	Adverse
BEP	Break-even point
BS	Balance sheet
B2B	Business-to-business
B2C	Business-to-customer
CA	Current assets
CL	Current liabilities
CM	Contribution margin
CoS	Cost of sales
CR	Creditor
DOP	Departmental operating profit
DR	Debtor
EPOS	Electronic point of sales
EPS	Earnings per share
F&B	Food and beverage
FAV	Favourable
FIFO	First in, first out
GM	General manager
GOP	Gross operating profit
GP	Gross profit
MBWA	Management by walking about
MSA	Motorway service area
NOP	Net operating profit
P&L	Profit and loss
PaT	Profit after tax
PbT	Profit before tax
P/E	Price/earnings (ratio)
PMS	Property management system
Rack rate	Full rate
REVPAR	Revenue per available room
REVPASH	Revenue per available seat hour
ROCE	Return on capital employed
USALI	Universal system of accounts for the lodging industry
VAT	Value Added Tax
ZBB	Zero based budgeting

Further resources

Books

Adams, D. (2006) *Management Accounting for the Hospitality Industry – a Strategic Approach*, 2nd edn, London: Thomson Learning.

Ashley, E. (2008) *Outsourcing for Dummies*, Chichester: Wiley.

Atfield, R. and Kemp, P. (2008) *Enhancing the International Learning Experience in Business and Management, Hospitality Leisure, Sport, Tourism*, Newbury: Threshold.

Atrill, P. and McLaney, E. (2008) *Financial Accounting for Non-Specialists*, 6th edn, Harlow: FT/Prentice Hall.

Barrows, C. and Powers, T. (2009) *Introduction to the Hospitality Industry*, 7th edn, Hoboken, NJ: Wiley.

Blyth, D. and Bruning, T. (2003) *Pubs, Bars and Clubs Handbook: Advice and Ideas for Running a Successful Licensed Business*, 6th edn, London: Kogan Page.

Boella, M. and Goss-Turner, S. (2005) *Human Resource Management in the Hospitality Industry: an Introductory Guide*, 8th edn, Oxford: Elsevier Butterworth-Heinemann.

Bowie, D. and Buttle, F. (2004) *Hospitality Marketing: an Introduction*, Oxford: Elsevier Butterworth-Heinemann.

British Hospitality Association (2009) *Hospitality Handbook*, available from hospitalityhandbook.com.

Brotherton, B. and Wood, R. (2008) *The SAGE Handbook of Hospitality Management*, London: Sage.

Cohen, M. and Bodeker, G. (2008) *Understanding the Global Spa Industry: Spa Management*, Oxford: Butterworth-Heinemann.

Cousins, J., Lillicrap, D. and Weekes, S. (2010) *Food and Beverage Service*, 8th edn, London: Hodder Education.

Davidson, A. (2008) *How to Understand the Financial Pages: A Guide to Money and the Jargon*, 2nd edn, London: Times/Kogan Page.

Davis, B., Lockwood, A., Pantelidis, I. and Alcott, P. (2008) *Food and Beverage Management*, 4th edn, Oxford: Butterworth-Heinemann.

Dittmer, P. and Keefe, D. (2006) *Principles of Food, Beverage and Labor Cost Controls*, 8th edn, New York: Van Nostrand Reinhold.

Drury, C. (2006) *Cost and Management Accounting: an Introduction*, 6th edn, London: Thomson.

Drury, C. (2009) *Management Accounting for Business*, 4th edn, London: Cengage Learning.

Feinstein, A. and Stefanelli, J. (2007) *Purchasing: Selection and Procurement for the Hospitality Industry*, Hoboken, NJ: J. Wiley.

Harris, P. (1999) *Profit Planning*, 2nd edn, Hospitality Managers' Pocket Books, Oxford: Butterworth-Heinemann.

Harris, P. and Mongiello, M. (eds) (2006) *Accounting and Financial Management: Developments in the International Hospitality Industry*, Oxford: Elsevier/Butterworth-Heinemann.

Hodgson, S. (2007) *The Times A–Z of Careers and Jobs*, 14th edn, London: Kogan Page.

Hospitality, Tourism, Leisure and Sport: CRAC Degree Course Guides, 2007/08, Series 1, Richmond: Trotman Education.

International Association of Hospitality Accountants (2006) *Uniform System of Accounts for the Lodging Industry*, 10th edn, Hotel Association of New York City.

Jagels, M. and Coltman, M. (2004) *Hospitality Management Accounting*, 8th edn, Hoboken, NJ: J. Wiley.

Kotler, P., Bowen, J. and Makens, J. (2009) *Marketing for Hospitality and Tourism*, 5th edn, Upper Saddle River, NJ: Pearson Education.

Krakhmal, V. and Harris, P. (2008) *Developing Customer Profitability Analysis for Hotels (Recommended Practice Guide)*, Wimbourne: British Association of Hospitality Accountants.

Larkin, E. (2009) *How to Run a Great Hotel: Everything You Need to Achieve Excellence in the Hotel Industry*, Oxford: How To Books.

Laser Directory of University and College Entry (2010), London: Trotman.

Lee-Ross, D. and Lashley, C. (2009) *Entrepreneurship and Small Business Management in the Hospitality Industry*, Oxford: Butterworth-Heinemann.

Miller, J., Dopson, L. and Hayes, D. (2008) *Food and Beverage Cost Control*, 4th edn, Chichester: Wiley .

Mudie, P. and Pirrie, A. (2006) *Services Marketing Management*, 3rd edn, Oxford: Butterworth-Heinemann.

Nickson, D. (2006) *Human Resource Management for the Hospitality and Tourism Industries*, Oxford: Butterworth-Heinemann.

Ninemeier, J. and Perdue, J. (2008) *Discovering Hospitality and Tourism: the World's Greatest Industry*, 2nd edn, Harlow: Pearson Prentice Hall.

Oxford Dictionary of Business and Management (2009) 5th edn, Oxford: Oxford University Press.

Pedler, R., Burgoyne, J. and Boydell, T. (2006) *A Manager's Guide to Self-Development*, 5th edn, London: McGraw Hill.

Pizam, A. (ed.) (2010) *International Encyclopedia of Hospitality Management*, 2nd edn, Oxford: Butterworth-Heinemann.

Ransley, J. and Ingram, H. (2004) *Developing Hospitality Property and Facilities*, Oxford: Butterworth-Heinemann.

Reid, W. and Myddelton, D. (2005) *The Meaning of Company Accounts*, 8th edn, Aldershot: Gower.

Sanders, E., Hill, T. and Faria, D. (2008) *Understanding Foodservice Cost Control: an Operational Text for Food, Beverage, and Labor Costs*, 3rd edn, Harlow: Prentice Hall

Slattery, P. (2009) *The Economic Ascent of the Hotel Business*, Oxford: Goodfellow Publishing.

Sloan, D. (2004) *Culinary Taste: Consumer Behaviour in the International Restaurant Sector*, Oxford: Elsevier Butterworth-Heinemann.

Tranter, K. (2009) *Introduction to Revenue Management for the Hospitality Industry: Principles and Practice for the Real World*, Upper Saddle River, NJ: Pearson Prentice-Hall.

TriHospitality (2010) *United Kingdom Hotel Industry 2010*, TriHospitality Consulting, London.

Vallen, G. and Vallen, J. (2009) *Check-in Check-out: Managing Hotel Operations*, 8th edn, Upper Saddle River, NJ: Pearson Prentice-Hall.

Van der Wagen, L. and Goonetilleke, A. (2004) *Hospitality Management: Strategy and Operations*, Frenchs Forest, NSW: Pearson.

Walker, J. and Lundberg, D. (2005) *The Restaurant: From Concept to Operation*, 4th edn, Hoboken, NJ: Wiley.

Waters, C. (2009) *Supply Chain Management: an Introduction to Logistics*, 2nd edn, Basingstoke: Palgrave Macmillan.

Journals and reports

Bottomline – the magazine of HFTP, Hotel Financial & Technology Professionals (US)

Caterer and Hotelkeeper

Industry trends

Travel and Tourism Intelligence Reports

Hospitality and tourism academic journals

Websites

aat.org.uk   Association of Accounting Technicians

abta.com   Association of British Travel Agents

accountingweb.com   Accounting information

acfws.co.uk   Academy of Food and Wine

ahla.com   American Hotel and Lodging Association

baha-uk.org.uk   British Association of Hospitality Accountants

bbc.co.uk/schools/bitesize   BBC site – really useful study advice, exercise practice, etc.

beerandpub.com   British Beer and Pubs Association

betterrevenue.com   Revenue Management news

bha.org.uk   British Hospitality Association

bii.org   British Institute of Innkeeping (qualifications and awards)

bis.gov.uk   Department for Business, Innovation and Skills

businesslink.gov.uk   Official government website for businesses of all sizes

caterer.com   Jobs in hospitality

catererandhotelkeeper.com   Caterer & Hotelkeeper magazine

cateringnet.co.uk   Catering network and directory

chme.co.uk   Council for Hospitality Management Education (UK)

chrie.org   Council for Hotel, Restaurant and Institutional Educators (US)

cim.co.uk   Chartered Institute of Marketing

cimaglobal.com   Chartered Institute of Management Accountants

cipd.co.uk   Chartered Institute of Personnel & Development

cips.org   Chartered Institute of Purchasing and Supply

culture.gov.uk   Department of Culture, Media & Sport

direct.gov.uk   Public services site (including higher education)

edexcel.com   EdExcel Foundation – education

environment-agency.gov.uk   Information on energy conservation

euromonitor.com   Leisure intelligence reports

fco.gov.uk   Foreign and Commonwealth office

fsb.org.uk   Federation of Small Businesses

ft.com   Financial Times – for financial data about hospitality

hftp.org   Hotel Financial & Technology Professionals (US)

hftp.org/HITEC   Hospitality industry technology association (US)

hospitalitynet.org   General hospitality site

hotcatuk.com   Networking site

hotel-online.com   General hospitality site

insolvencyhelpline.co.uk   Advice for businesses in financial difficulty

instituteofhospitality.org   Institute of hospitality – qualifications, resources, networking

ilam.co.uk   Institute of Leisure Amenity Management

www.ism.ws   Institute for Supply Management

laca.org.uk   Local Authority Caterers Organisation

london2012.com   The London 2012 Olympics official site

londonstockexchange.com   The London Stock Exchange

mia-uk.com   Meetings Industry Association

mintel.com   Leisure intelligence reports

netregs.gov.uk   Environmental guidance for business site

people1st.co.uk   Sector skills council

restaurateursguide.com   Restaurant Association of Great Britain

savoyeducationaltrust.org.uk   Charity trust fund for helping with payment for education and training

smallbusiness.co.uk   Advice for small businesses

springboarduk.net   Springboard industry careers organisation

statistics.gov.uk   Hub site for UK national statistics

theaccu.co.uk   Association of Contract Catering Users

thebfa.org   British Franchise Association

trihospitality.com   Reports on industry trends

uk.reuters.com   Reuters news agency

ukparks.com   British Holiday and Home Park Association

wiredhotelier.com   General hospitality site

world-tourism.org   UN World tourism

wttc.com   World Travel and Tourism Council

And those of any company

Developing skills

Answers to the Exercises

Chapter 2

Exercise 2.1 (Pub P&L)

	Actual (£)	Actual (%)	Budget (£)	Budget (%)	Variance (£)	Variance (%)
Food and beverage						
Sales	12,000	100.0	12,500	100.0	(500)	(4.0)
Cost of sales	(3,800)	(31.7)	(3,800)	(30.4)	0	0.0
Gross profit	8,200	68.3	8,700	69.6	(500)	(5.7)
Payroll	(2,700)	(22.5)	(2,700)	(21.6)	0	0.0
Benefits	(500)	(4.2)	(500)	(4.0)	0	0.0
Departmental expenses	(1,600)	(13.3)	(1,600)	(12.8)	0	0.0
Departmental profit	3,400	28.3	3,900	31.2	(500)	(12.8)
Accommodation						
Sales	1,900	100.0	1,950	100.0	(50)	(2.6)
Payroll	(400)	(21.1)	(400)	(20.5)	0	0.0
Benefits	(80)	(4.2)	(80)	(4.1)	0	0.0
Departmental expenses	(200)	(10.5)	(200)	(10.3)	0	0.0
Departmental profit	1,220	64.2	1,270	65.1	(50)	(3.9)
Administration						
Admin. expenses	1,100	7.9	1,100	7.6	0	0.0
Maintenance	100	0.7	100	0.7	0	0.0
Total	1,200	8.6	1,200	8.3	0	0.0
Fixed charges						
Rates	500	3.6	500	3.5	0	0.0
Depreciation	1,400	10.1	1,400	9.7	0	0.0
Total	1,900	13.7	1,900	13.1	0	0.0
Front page P&L	(£)	(%)	(£)	(%)	(£)	(%)
Sales – F&B	12,000	86.3	12,500	86.5	(500)	(4.0)
Sales – accommodation	1,900	13.7	1,950	13.5	(50)	(2.6)
Total sales	13,900	100.0	14,450	100.0	(550)	(3.8)
Cost of sales	(3,800)	(27.3)	(3,800)	(26.3)	0	0.0
Gross profit	10,100	72.7	10,650	73.7	(550)	(5.2)
Departmental payroll	(3,100)	(22.3)	(3,100)	(21.5)	0	0.0
Departmental benefits	(580)	(4.2)	(580)	(4.0)	0	0.0
Departmental expenses	(1,800)	(12.9)	(1,800)	(12.5)	0	0.0
Departmental profit	4,620	33.2	5,170	35.8	(550)	(10.6)
Administration costs	(1,200)	(8.6)	(1,200)	(8.3)	0	0.0
Gross operating profit	3,420	24.6	3,970	27.5	(550)	(13.9)
Fixed charges	(1,900)	(13.7)	(1,900)	(13.1)	0	0.0
Net profit	1,520	10.9	2,070	14.3	(550)	(26.6)

Exercise 2.2

	Assets	Liabilities
Point of sale system	√	
Mortgage		√
Delivery van	√	
Staff accommodation that is owned	√	
Stocks of frozen food	√	
Phone units used but not paid for		√
Yearly rental on coffee machine, paid in advance	√	
Amount owing from a customer	√	
Overdraft		√
Amount owing to a supplier		√

Did you get them right? Can you think of any more in your area?

Exercise 2.3

	Assets (£)		Capital (£)		Liabilities (£)
A	2,800	=	**700**	+	2,100
B	285	=	226	+	**59**
C	52,000	=	**31,400**	+	20,600
D	**4,900**	=	3,400	+	1,500

Exercise 2.4

		= Net value (£)
Fixed assets		
Equipment		22,000
Current assets		
Debtors	7,650	
Stocks	1,150	
Cash	1,700	
Total current assets	10,500	
Less current liabilities		
Creditors	(4,300)	
Total current liabilities	(4,300)	
= Working capital		6,200
Net assets total		28,200
Financed by		
Profit		1,200
Capital for year		27,000
Total		28,200

Exercise 2.5

	(£)
Opening stock (as at the start of the period)	490
Plus purchases	11,060
=	11,550
Minus cost of staff meals	(920)
Minus closing stock	(530)
= Cost of sales	10,100

Exercise 2.6

	(£)
Rental (per year)	10,400
Charge per 4 weekly period is (divide by 13)	800
Eight periods amortised on the P&L	6,400
Five periods remaining on the BS	4,000

Exercise 2.7

Item	Cost	Depreciation rate	Amount	Net (at end year 1)
Equipment	£6,800	10%	£680	£6,120
Furniture	£2,600	20%	£520	£2.080

Exercise 2.8

Workings out

Depreciation	Rate	Value (£)	Depreciation (£)
Equipment	10%	10,200	1,020
Furniture	15%	3,900	585
Total		14,100	1,605

Prepayment	Value (£)	Prepay (£)	Net (£)
Rates	870	174	696
Marketing	300	60	240
Total		234	936

Accrual	Value (£)	Accrue	Net (£)
Utilities	1,395	342	1,737
Payroll	8,835	90	8,925
Total		432	10,662

Cost of sales calculation

	(£)
Opening stock	738
Plus purchases	16,482
Less staff meals	(1,380)
Less closing stock	(804)
Equals cost of sales (CoS)	15,036

Profit & Loss Report

	(£)	(%)
Sales	39,852	100.0
Less cost of sales	(15,036)	(37.7)
Gross profit	24,816	62.3
Less payroll	(8,925)	(22.4)
	15,891	39.9

Less other expenses		
Utilities	(1,737)	(4.4)
Marketing	(240)	(0.6)
Repairs & maintenance	(1,275)	(3.2)
Staff meals	(1,380)	(3.5)
Laundry	(1,239)	(3.1)
Miscellaneous	(3,528)	(8.9)
Total	(9,399)	(23.6)
Gross operating profit	6,492	16.3
Less fixed charges		
Depreciation	(1,605)	(4.0)
Rates	(696)	(1.7)
Total	(2,301)	(5.8)
Net profit	4,191	10.5

Balance Sheet

Fixed assets	Gross (£)	Depreciation (£)	Net (£)
Buildings	18,000		18,000
Equipment	10,200	(1,020)	9,180
Furniture	3,900	(585)	3,315
China, glass & silver	1,500		1,500
Total			31,995
Current assets			
Cash	3,000		
Floats	60		
Stocks	804		
Prepayments	234		
Debtors	1,560		
Total current assets	5,658		
Current liabilities			
Creditors	2,520		
Accruals	432		
Total current liabilities	2,952		
Working capital			2,706
Net assets			34,701
Financed by			
Capital			33,510
Plus net profit			4,191
Less drawings			(3,000)
Total			34,701

Chapter 3

Exercise 3.1

Rooms sold		Occupancy (%)
Rack rate	5	5.6
Leisure	10	11.1
Business	60	66.7
	75	83.3

Rooms revenue	Total	Average room rate (£)
Rack rate	£550	110.00
Leisure	£650	65.00
Business	£6,000	100.00
Total	£7,200	96.00

Exercise 3.2

Profit & Loss Report – Restaurant: 28-day period

	Budget		Actual		Variance	
Seats available per day	50		50			
Seats per 28-day period	1,400		1,400		0	0.0
Covers sold	1,120		952		(168)	(15.0)
Sales	(£)	(%)	(£)	(%)	(£)	(%)
Food	20,100	75.0	17,600	80.4	(2,500)	(12.4)
Beverage	6,700	25.0	4,300	19.6	(2,400)	(35.8)
Total	26,800	100.0	21,900	100.0	(4,900)	(18.3)
Average spend/cover – food £p	17.95		18.49		0.54	3.0
Average spend/cover – beverage £p	5.98		4.52		(1.47)	(24.5)
Seat occupancy %	80.0		68.0		(12.0)	(15.0)

So – what does it mean? Here are a few comments:

Customers – Seat occupancy is down by 15% – this means that, with an average of 34 seats occupied a day, 16 aren't sold. Can you identify why this is? Are any particular days worse than others are?

Average spend for food is up on budget, but beverage is down – so you should add the two together. This gives an overall actual of £23.01 whereas the budget was £23.93 – down almost 4%. Do you know why? Was the budget wrong (easy to say yes, with hindsight – but why did you set it as this)?

Together (occupancy and spend) means a shortfall of almost £5,000 on revenue – 18%. Is there anything happening locally that would affect both of these factors? If you can identify why things have gone wrong then perhaps you can do something about it.

Exercise 3.3

		July	August	September
Days in month		23	22	22
		(£)	(£)	(£)
Sales	Deli-bar	19,200	15,000	22,875
	Food hall	39,750	33,750	59,250
	Total	58,950	48,750	82,125
Covers	Deli-bar	5,200	4,200	5,900
	Food hall	8,300	7,600	12,300
	Total	13,500	11,800	18,200
Covers per day	Deli-bar	226	191	268
	Food hall	361	345	559
	Total	587	536	827
		(£p)	(£p)	(£p)
Average spends	Deli-bar	3.69	3.57	3.88
	Food hall	4.79	4.44	4.82
	Total	4.37	4.13	4.51
		(£)	(£)	(£)
Sales per day	Deli-bar	835	682	1,040
	Food hall	1,728	1,534	2,693
	Total	2,563	2,216	3,733

What can you work out from these numbers? What's the trend in customers and spends?

Chapter 4

Exercise 4.1: Restaurant

	Budget		Actual		Variance	Var %
Seats available	50		50			
Seats per period	1,400		1,400		0	0.0
Covers sold	1,120		952		(168)	(15.0)
	(£)	(%)	(£)	(%)	(£)	(%)
Sales						
Food	20,100	75.0	17,600	80.4	(2,500)	(12.4)
Beverage	6,700	25.0	4,300	19.6	(2,400)	(35.8)
Total	26,800	100.0	21,900	100.0	(4,900)	(18.3)

Cost of sales						
Food	(10,000)	(49.8)	(7,900)	(44.9)	2,100	21.0
Beverage	(2,670)	(39.9)	(1,620)	(37.7)	1,050	39.3
Total	(12,670)	(47.3)	(9,520)	(43.5)	3,150	24.9
Gross profit						
Food	10,100	50.2	9,700	55.1	(400)	(4.0)
Beverage	4,030	60.1	2,680	62.3	(1,350)	(33.5)
Total	14,130	52.7	12,380	56.5	(1,750)	(12.4)
Payroll cost	(9,520)	(35.5)	(8,400)	(38.4)	1,120	11.7
Departmental expenses	(2,100)	(7.8)	(1,600)	(7.3)	500	23.8
Food & beverage profit	2,510	9.4	2,380	10.9	(130)	(5.2)
	(£)		(£)		(£)	(%)
Average spend/cover – food	17.95		18.49		0.54	3.0
Average spend/cover – beverage	5.98		4.52		(1.47)	(24.5)
Total cost of sales/cover	11.31		10.00		(1.31)	(11.6)
Total gross profit/cover	12.62		13.00		0.39	3.1
Payroll cost per cover	8.50		8.82		0.32	(3.8)
Expenses cost per cover	1.88		1.68		0.19	(10.4)
Profit per cover	2.24		2.50		0.26	11.6
Seat occupancy %	80.0		68.0		(12.0)	(15.0)

What do all these figures mean? Look at these:

☐ Is there any relationship between the average spends for food and for beverage?

☐ What about the cost of food amounts? The average costs look less, but what about the percentage?

☐ Is payroll cost 'good' or 'bad' – and from whose perspective? Is there a relationship between payroll and cost of sales, for instance?

☐ What about other expenses?

☐ Lastly, what about profit?

Exercise 4.2: Town centre department store

	March		April		May	
	(£)	(%)	(£)	(%)	(£)	(%)
Sales						
Cafe	9,000	42.9	10,500	41.2	12,000	36.4
Restaurant	12,000	57.1	15,000	58.8	21,000	63.6
Total	21,000	100.0	25,500	100.0	33,000	100.0
Cost of sales						

Cafe	(4,500)	50.0	(5,670)	54.0	(6,840)	57.0
Restaurant	(4,800)	40.0	(6,300)	42.0	(9,030)	43.0
Total	(9,300)	44.3	(11,970)	46.9	(15,870)	48.1
Gross profit						
Cafe	4,500	50.0	4,830	46.0	5,160	43.0
Restaurant	7,200	60.0	8,700	58.0	11,970	57.0
Total	11,700	55.7	13,530	53.1	17,130	51.9
Wages	(5,250)	25.0	(5,860)	23.0	(4,485)	13.6
Overtime	(450)	2.1	(530)	2.1	(2,115)	6.4
Net profit	6,000	28.6	7,140	28.0	10,530	31.9
Covers						
Cafe	3,750		4,667		5,714	
Restaurant	1,667		2,128		3,043	
Total	5,417		6,795		8,757	
	(£)		(£)		(£)	
Average spends						
Cafe	2.40		2.25		2.10	
Restaurant	7.20		7.05		6.90	
Total	3.88		3.75		3.77	
Gross profit/cover						
Cafe	1.20		1.03		0.90	
Restaurant	4.32		4.09		3.93	
Total	2.16		1.99		1.96	
Wages/cover	0.97		0.86		0.51	
Overtime/cover	0.08		0.08		0.24	
Net profit/cover	1.11		1.05		1.20	

By the way – the total average spend is the total revenue divided by total covers. It's not calculated by averaging the two spends as you can't 'average an average'. That's why it might look slightly odd.

Where do you start with your analysis? Look at the trends in sales – customers and spends – and compare month to month . There's a rise in covers as you move towards summer – what does this tell you about the location?

Look at the changes in both CoS and payroll % (basic and OT). Could they be linked? What is happening here?

The most likely scenario is that a lack of staff ('HR issue') is resulting in more purchasing of ready-prepared foods (leading to higher CoS – 'F&B issue'). As a result, you would also have to consider the morale and health of staff (are they overworked?) and the implications of this (are they giving the best service?) and so on. Again, you need to take a holistic approach here.

Chapter 5

Exercise 5.1

Coffees		5,000
	Total	Per cup
	(£)	(£)
Fixed costs	5,000	1.00
Profit required	1,250	0.25
Variable costs		
Food		0.25
Labour		0.20
Paper		0.07
Add all these together to get a selling price		1.77
Add the VAT (multiply by 1.2)		2.12

You could check it works by multiplying it all out to see if you reach the profit that you require.

	(£)
Sales	8,850
Variable costs	(2,600)
Contribution	6,250
Fixed costs	(5,000)
Net profit	1,250

Now you can see why good cups of coffee are so expensive!

Exercise 5.2

If contribution is 45% then variable costs are 45%:

$$\frac{\text{Variable cost £}}{\text{Variable cost \%}} = \frac{£32.45}{55\%} = £59.00 \text{ selling price} = £70.80 \text{ inc VAT (say £71?)}$$

Exercise 5.3

Rooms available	27,740	365 days per year
Rooms sold	19,418	70% occupancy
	(£)	
Profit required	980,000	then add back tax
= Income before tax	1,361,111	(check tax £381,111 28%)
Fixed costs	600,000	
Administration costs	435,000	
Departmental operating profit	2,396,111	
Less F&B & other dept profit	(200,000)	
= Rooms profit	2,196,111	

Rooms expenses	394,185	£20.30 cost times rooms sold
Rooms revenue required	2,590,297	
	(£p)	
Average room rate	133.40	revenue divided by rooms sold
Rate plus VAT	160.08	@ 20%

Exercise 5.4

Information and workings out

Average spend	£ 43.00	Return on investment	15%
Cost of sales	32%		
Other variable costs	15%	Furniture and equipment	£4,500,000
Salaries	£750,000	Depreciation (years)	10
Rent and rates	£700,000	Depreciation per year	£450,000
Insurance	£80,000		
Administration	£120,000	days in year	365

Fixed costs	(£)	Contribution margin	(£)	(%)
Salaries	750,000	Selling price	43.00	100.0
Rent and rates	700,000	Cost of sales	(13.76)	(32.0)
Insurance	80,000	Other variable costs	(6.45)	(15.0
Administration	120,000	= total variable costs	(20.21)	(47.0)
Depreciation	450,000			
Total fixed costs	2,100,000	Contribution Margin	22.79	53.0

Answer

$$\frac{\text{Fixed costs}}{\text{Contribution margin}} \quad \frac{£2,100,000}{£22.79} = 92,146 \text{ covers total or 252.5 per day}$$

$$\frac{\text{Investment}}{\text{Return required}} \quad \frac{£4,500,000}{15\%} = £675,000 \text{ profit required (which} = 15\% \text{ of the £4.5m)}$$

$$\frac{\text{Fixed costs} + \text{profit required}}{\text{Contribution margin}} \quad \frac{£2,775,000}{£22.79} = 121,764 \text{ covers total or 333.6 per day}$$

This assumes that it is open every day of the year. What if it were not? Then the average per day would be different. You could try it for, say, 350 days.

Exercise 5.5

First you need to find out the number of extra visitors

Workings out

Extra visitors	June	July	August	Total
total days	30	31	31	
Weekend days	8	8	8	
Weekdays	22	23	23	
Visitors – weekend (40 per day)	320	320	320	
Visitors – weekday (25 per day)	550	575	575	
Total extra visitors	870	895	895	2,660

Then you need to find out the costs

Total existing visitors	6,500
	(£)
Total variable costs for existing visitors (£4,000+£890+£1,750)	6,640
Cost per existing visitor	1.02
Extra variable costs per new visitor	3.25
Total variable cost per new visitor	4.27
Additional fixed cost (advertising) per new visitor	0.64
(£1,700 divided by 2,660 new visitors)	
Total cost per new visitor	4.91

Selling price

Profit % required 30%, therefore Total cost % =70%. Use grossing up technique to find selling price.

$$\text{Selling price} \quad = \quad \frac{\text{Cost £}}{\text{Cost \%}} \quad = \quad \frac{£4.91}{70\ \%} \quad = £7.01$$

Break-even point

Contribution per unit	(£)
Selling price	7.01
Variable costs per new visitor	(4.27)
Contribution per new visitor	2.74

BEP

$$\frac{\text{Fixed costs (advertising)}}{\text{Contribution/unit}} \quad \frac{£1,700}{£2.74} = 620 \text{ visitors}$$

Effect on profit for 3-month period

	Existing	New	Total	
Visitors	19,500	2,660	22,160	
	(£)	(£)	(£)	(%)
Sales (Visitors × rate)	107,250	18,660	125,910	100.0
Variable costs	(19,920)	(11,362)	(31,282)	24.8
Contribution	87,330	7,298	94,628	75.2
Fixed costs	(55,000)	(1,700)	(56,700)	45.0
Profit	32,330	5,598	37,928	30.1

Chapter 6

Exercise 6.1

	Normal	Down 20%	Up 20%
Rooms sold	10	8	12
Average rate	£80.00	£80.00	£80.00
Breakfast cost per room	£5.00	£5.00	£5.00
Supplies cost per room	£18.00	£18.00	£18.00
Fixed costs	£210	£210	£210
	£	£	£
Sales	800	640	960
Food cost	(50)	(40)	(60)
Staff & supplies	(180)	(144)	(216)
Fixed costs	(210)	(210)	(210)
Profit	360	246	474

Exercise 6.2

	Occupancy normal	Occupancy down 20%, costs up 5%	Occupancy up 20%, costs up 5%
	£	£	£
Sales	800	640	960
Food cost	(50)	(42)	(63)
Staff & supplies	(180)	(151)	(227)
Fixed costs	(210)	(221)	(221)
Profit	360	226	450

So if occupancy is down by 20%, and costs rise by 5%, profits drop by 37% (360 less 226 = 134, expressed as a percentage of 360).

It doesn't look much for such a small business but imagine if it were 50 times bigger.

Exercise 6.3

	Original percentage	Original (£)	Mailshot (£)	Equipment (£)
Sales	100.0	600,000	60,000	50,000
F&B costs	(40.0)	(240,000)	(24,000)	(20,000)
Gross profit	60.0	360,000	36,000	30,000
Less payroll (variable)	(20.0)	(120,000)	(12,000)	(10,000)
Less other variable costs	(8.0)	(48,000)	(4,800)	(4,000)
Contribution	32.0	192,000	19,200	16,000
Less fixed payroll	(10.0)	(60,000)		
Less other fixed costs	(20.0)	(120,000)		
Mailshot costs			(1,000)	
Equipment costs				(20,000)
Profit	2.0	12,000	18,200	(4,000)

(You could also work out revised percentages)

Exercise 6.4

Workings out

Forecast sales	£420,000	
Shortfall	20%	
So the forecast =	80%	(of budget)
Therefore, budget sales are	£525,000	Using grossing up technique

	Budget (%)	Budget (£)	Forecast (£)	Variance (£)	Variance (%)
Total sales	100.0%	525,000	420,000	(105,000)	(20.0)
Less food & beverage costs	37.0%	(194,250)	(155,400)	38,850	(20.0)
Less wages (variable)	19.5%	(102,375)	(81,900)	20,475	(20.0)
Less variable expenses	4.5%	(23,625)	(18,900)	4,725	(20.0)
= Contribution	39.0%	204,750	163,800	(40,950)	(20.0)
Less salaries	9.0%	(47,250)	(47,250)	0	0.0
Less other fixed costs	20.0%	(105,000)	(105,000)	0	0.0
= Net Profit	10.0%	52,500	11,550	(40,950)	(78.0)

The same variable cost percentages are applied to the new sales, meaning that the contribution % is the same as budget (39.0%). However, as the fixed costs don't change the result is a 78% drop in profits compared to the 20% drop in sales. If this were your situation you would have to see if you could do something about the sales, but also anything about the fixed costs.

Chapter 8

Exercise 8.1

Ingredient F		(£)	
Standard quantity × standard price	255 × £2.00 =	510.00	
Actual quantity × standard price	265.2 × £2.00 =	530.40	
Quantity variance		20.40	ADV
Actual quantity × actual price	265.2 × £1.90 =	503.88	
Price variance		26.52	FAV
(difference between ACTQ SP and ACTQ AP)			
Total variance ingredient F		6.12	FAV
Ingredient O			
Standard quantity × standard price	127.5 × £2.40 =	306.00	
Actual quantity × standard price	178.5 × £2.40 =	428.40	
Quantity variance		122.40	ADV
Actual quantity × actual price	178.5 × £2.60 =	464.10	
Price variance		35.70	ADV
Total variance ingredient O		158.10	ADV
Total variances for recipe (F + O)		151.98	ADV

Can you identify where the major problem has occurred?

It's the ingredient O and is in the actual quantity used – but the price is a problem too. The quantity of ingredient F increased a little but compensated by costing slightly less per kilogram.

Exercise 8.2

Catering assistants		(£)	
budget hours × budget rate	120 × £7.00 =	840	
actual hours × budget rate	110 × £7.00 =	770	
		70	FAV
actual hours × actual rate	110 × £7.10 =	781	
		11	ADV
Total		59	FAV
General assistants			
budget hours × budget rate	160 × £6.50 =	1,040	
actual hours × budget rate	170 × £6.50 =	1,105	
		65	ADV
actual hours × actual rate	170 × £6.40 =	1,088	
		17	FAV
Total		48	ADV
Total variance		11	FAV

Exercise 8.3

	Covers	Selling price (£)	Sales (£)	
Budget	3,320	6.75	22,410.00	
Actual	3,170	6.80	21,556.00	
Variance	(150)	0.05	854.00	ADV
Volume (usage)	(150)	6.75	1,012.50	ADV
Price	3,170	0.05	158.50	FAV
Total			854.00	ADV

Exercise 8.4

	Rooms	Selling price (£)	Sales £	
Budget	50	79.50	3,975.00	
Actual	55	77.50	4,262.50	
Variance	5	(2.00)	287.50	FAV
Volume (usage)	5	79.50	397.50	FAV
Price	55	(2.00)	110.00	ADV
Total			287.50	FAV

Chapter 10

Exercise 10.1

Ordinary shares	Called-up share capital	£250,000
	Number or ordinary shares	500,000
	So the nominal price of each is	£0.50

$$\text{Return on capital employed} = \frac{\text{Profit before interest and tax}}{\text{Net assets}} = \frac{£275,000}{£418,000} = 65.8\%$$

$$\text{Gross profit} = \frac{\text{Gross profit}}{\text{Sales (Turnover)}} = \frac{£465,000}{£1,875,000} = 24.8\%$$

$$\text{Profitability} = \frac{\text{Profit before interest and tax}}{\text{Sales}} = \frac{£275,000}{£1,875,000} = 14.7\%$$

$$\text{Gearing} = \frac{\text{Debt}}{\text{Equity}} = \frac{£340,000}{£418,000} = 81.3\%$$

$$\text{Liquidity – Current ratio} = \frac{\text{Current assets}}{\text{Current liabilities}} = \frac{£685,000}{£437,000} = 1.57:1$$

$$\text{Liquidity – Acid test} = \frac{\text{Debtors + cash}}{\text{Current liabilities}} = \frac{£310,000}{£437,000} = 0.71:1$$

Earnings per share	$=$	$\dfrac{\text{Profit after tax}}{\text{No. Issued ordinary shares}}$	$=$ $=$	£168,000 500,000	$=$	£0.34
Dividend per share	$=$	$\dfrac{\text{Ordinary dividend paid}}{\text{No. issued ordinary shares}}$	$=$ $=$	£100,000 500,000	$=$	£0.20
Price earnings ratio	$=$	$\dfrac{\text{Market price per share}}{\text{Earnings per share}}$	$=$ $=$	£1.50 £0.34	$=$	4.46 :1
Debtor days	$=$	$\dfrac{\text{Debtors}}{\text{Average sales per day}}$	$=$	£250,000 £5,137	$=$	48.67 days

(If you had prior year figures you could also have compared these figures to those.)

Index

E

Earnings per share   196
Education   8
Electronic point of sale (EPOS)   54, 71, 129
Employee benefits   78
E-pay   134
Event catering   49

F

Fast food   5
Financed By section   32
Financial accounts   20
Financial control   14
Financial controller   15
Financial skills   206, 209, 210
Fixed assets   30
Fixed charges   23, 82
Fixed costs   65, 81
Fixed liabilities   31
Fixed payroll   74
Flexible payroll   76
Floats   127
Food and beverage controller   16
Food cost percentage   69
Forces catering   9
Forecasting   76, 106
Forecasting cash   118
Forecasting new products   115
Forecasting process   108
Forecasting profits   112
Forecasting spreadsheets   175
Forecasting volumes   110
Foreign exchange   129
Franchising   200
Fraud   11
Front page P&L   25
Function or event catering   8
Further resources   207

G

Gearing   197
General cashier   15
Gross operating profit   23
Gross profit   23
Gross profit pricing   87
Grossing up   89
Guest laundry   73

H

Hospitals   8
Hotels   4
Hubbart formula   90

I

Incentive schemes   53
Increasing customers   54
Increasing spends   53
Industry, features   3
Input and output   165
In-room entertainment   73
Inventory   144

L

Labour cost   73
Leisure centres   7
Liabilities   30
Life span   115
Limited companies   188
Limiting factors   117
Line charts   177, 182
Liquidity   125
Long term investments   30
Loss leader   93, 95

M

Management   11
Management accounts   20, 190
Management contracts   201
Managing costs   81
Market segments   29, 39
Market segments – spreadsheets   176
Market-based pricing   94
Markets, captive   40
MBWA   41, 71
Menu engineering   72
Menu fatigue   54
Menu price   87
Month end   16
Motorway service areas   6
Mystery shoppers   56, 72
Net profit   23, 31

N

Non-profit organizations   98
Notes to the Accounts   192